W9-ACV-452

ESSAYS ON MUSIC

Andrew A. Fraser

ESSAYS ON MUSIC

By

ANDREW A. FRASER

Essay Index Reprint Series

BOOKS FOR LIBRARIES PRESS, INC.
FREEPORT, NEW YORK

First Published 1930
Reprinted 1968

LIBRARY OF CONGRESS CATALOG CARD NUMBER:
68-16932

PRINTED IN THE UNITED STATES OF AMERICA

PREFACE

ANDREW FRASER passed away on 8th June 1929 at Montana, Switzerland, after a short illness contracted through an over-strenuous winter's work in Berlin. Born in Madras in 1901, he was educated at the Edinburgh Academy on the classical side, and at Balliol College, Oxford (1919–23), where he read history and took his degree. On going down he spent two years with Messrs. W. & R. Chambers, publishers in Edinburgh, and wrote many of the articles on artistic subjects in the new edition of their Encyclopaedia. The paramount interest in his life was music, and feeling that he had scarcely found his right niche, he gave up this post and decided to devote himself to musical journalism. The high standards which he set himself demanded a thorough-going technical education in music, in addition to the liberal education that he already possessed. Accordingly he determined to study music seriously abroad, and intermingle this with foreign travel adapted to artistic pursuits. It was while so engaged that fatal illness overtook him, and a life of extraordinary promise was suddenly cut off.

He studied the organ while at school, but the years of the War naturally cramped musical activity in the wider sense. Thus Fraser, partly from outside circumstances and partly from his own natural reserve and reticence, did not find himself until he went to Oxford. There he discovered an outlet for his enthusiasms and activities in such organizations as the Balliol College Musical Society, of which he became secretary, the O. U. French Club, and others. While there he made the discovery too, as have others in their time, that an interest in art, music, or literature does not imply social ostracism, nor the cultivation of the Muses a suspected obscurity.

On his return to Edinburgh he founded the still active Terpander Club, a society for producing and studying modern musical compositions, open alike to professional and amateur musicians; and became a member of the Speculative Society in Edinburgh University. Besides these activities he found time to write many articles on musical subjects which appeared from time to time in various periodicals, such as the *Chesterian, Musical Opinion,* and *Music and Letters*; it is a selection of these which will be found in this volume.

In the past it has been a commonplace to say that the musician is a specialist—and a specialist of the worst kind—in that he knows little and cares less for things outside his own art. Such criticism is rapidly becoming unjustifiable. Fraser represents to some extent this new movement in music; for to it he brought a mind trained on the classics, widened by an intimacy with French and German literature, stimulated by a familiarity with the painting, architecture, and sculpture of all schools; and last, but not least, a mind supported by those sterling qualities of character that are the glory of Scotland. Intolerance of shams, devotion to ideals, and finely finished work; these three sum up Fraser's attitude to life.

In music his interests and sympathies lay largely with the most recent developments of the art both on the Continent and in England. His knowledge of works written in the present century was extensive, though he fully realized that a proper judgement of them was impossible without a grounding in the musical classics, and at least a passing acquaintance with folk-music. It is noticeable that in writing about recent composers, he sought to analyse their environment, both artistic and non-artistic, as an aid to understanding their works. Thus he seeks to show that architecture, literature, economic conditions, natural scenery, industrialism, political theory may one or all have some effect on the composer, and consequently none must be omitted in a serious study.

In a word music is not isolated from the complex web of modern life, but is, in part at least, a product and reflection of it.

The adequate presentation of such a point of view presupposes a wide diversity of interests, a mastery of facts, a quickness to grasp analogies, a power of distinguishing the relevant from the irrelevant, and finally a gift of expression. Those who read the following pages will find abundant proof of such qualities.

C. I. ANDERSON.

EDINBURGH,
April 1930.

CONTENTS

ESSAYS ON MUSIC

WAGNER AND SYMBOLISM

(*March* 1923)

M. ROMAIN ROLLAND has written somewhere that Wagner's 'works are epic symphonies. As a frame for them I should like temples; as scenery, the illimitable land of thought; as actors our dreams.' A pleasing fancy, yet a crushing criticism. Wagner—the man whose artistic life was so bound up with the theatre, who disliked extracts from his works to be given at concerts, who wished to keep *Parsifal* pure and guileless at Bayreuth! The man who claimed to renew the Greek tragedy, and to make it even more perfect by the co-ordination of all the arts into one harmonious whole! It was a Sisyphean task, and his was a failure; but it was a glorious one, a failure of necessity.

That the arts can be really co-ordinated is a practical impossibility. There is the great dividing line between painting and sculpture, which are static, and poetry and music, which are continuous. Music can aid poetry, and poetry can serve as inspiration for music, with some hope of success; but when a painter comes to deal with a poem or story he has but two alternatives—he can take one episode, perhaps the most salient or the most attractive, or else he can make a semi-imaginary creation embodying some or all of the characters concerned, and casting over the whole the same atmosphere as the writer casts over the story or poem. (A primitive may tell a story depicted in different little scenes, all on the same canvas, but that is hardly a fair example.) Even with two arts possessing so much in common as music and poetry, the technique, the form, the focus of interest, the treatment and nature of the climax—all these are different, and much more so when comparison is made with painting or sculpture.

Art is primarily a means of self-expression, and the medium chosen varies according to the character of the artist. Extreme versatility has not so far existed among men of genius that they have excelled in all branches. Even Leonardo, despite his flute-playing, his diaries, and his philosophizing, was first and foremost a painter, as far as art is concerned. Wagner himself is a proof. His verse is only fair, his prose is stiff, and his ideas on pictorial art as exemplified by his stage directions are crude in the extreme. One of the most exquisite symbolists in music, he seemed to have had little idea of symbolism in art. True it was he used his plots with a marvellous cunning. The grotto of Venus, the castle of Montsalvat, the gold from the Rhine, Klingsor's magic garden of flowers—they are all more than stage illusions, they are metaphors for life's experience; but the paraphernalia of the 'Ring' is carried to an absurdity. What is the use of asking for the maidens swimming in the Rhine, or Fafner speaking in the guise of a dragon, or the Valkyries sweeping through the clouds, when such things are beyond the possibilities of human endeavour? Supernatural elements on a large scale can be introduced on the stage as a pantomime joke, or personified into something tangible. Wagner demands the real thing, or at least the best imitation, and here 's the rub. Suggestion, not imitation, is the fundamental truth of art, and it is folly to talk of the union of the arts if glorious music be coupled with moderate words and indifferent scenery, which as often as not varies with the different theatres. (Incidentally, apart from *Tannhäuser* and *Parsifal*, where does the Greek dance disappear to?)

Take, for example, the Prelude to the *Rheingold*, or Wotan's Abschied. Why mock our eyes, when the orchestra is playing some of the divinest music Wagner ever wrote? For this reason *Tristan und Isolde* is undoubtedly his most perfect work. There are no distractions, and the scenery can be, comparatively speaking, of the simplest. The characters in the drama might live in any age, in any clime. Tristan and Isolde are themselves mere symbols. A man and a woman meet; they love; they die. It is the tragedy of life made naked, stark. Nor are they mere Pétrouchkian puppets or Mélisandian shadows; they are human beings, but human beings, so to speak, in the abstract. The type is delineated from the individual, but at the same time the interests of individuality are still retained. Butterfly's childlike faith, Canio's sarcastic anguish—it would be easy to collect instances from operatic literature of all kinds. The link between the literary and the musical aspects of the music drama is of course the *leit-motif*, itself a symbol, and where Wagner allows his literary side to predominate he becomes tire-some. Each of his operas has a bore—the Land-grave, Wotan, Sachs, King Mark, Gurnemanz, and argumentative reality suddenly appears. It is all right in *Louise*, Montmartre being such as it is, but when we enter a mythological land, a land of gnomes and nymphs and giants and gods of mystic rites and chivalresque endeavours, we feel we should like to stay there. Wagner as a musician is another affair altogether; what more exquisite than the Siegfried Idyll, than—— But one must stop. Throw aside all the lumbering books about the drama of the future, all the jargon about Art and the Greeks, forget the impossible actors and the tawdry theatre, and listen expectant, exultant, to the music!

MUSIC AND MORALITY

(1925)

MUSIC is perhaps the most universal art. Given adequate conditions, it can be performed in a similar manner all over the world, while a painting can only be shown in one place at a time, and a masterpiece of literature can never be the same in a translation. It is the art which makes the most direct appeal. Whether it is, that sound is the oldest form of expression, that the earliest beings who inhabited this earth first communicated with each other by sounds, it is inexpedient for the moment to discuss, but the fact remains that the march and the rag-time penetrate even deeper than the spectacular revue or the sentimental novelette. Finally, it is in Music that we have the most complete identification of what the composer has to say with the manner in which he says it, as the medium is so essentially specialized. We have words ready to hand before the coming of the poet, and landscapes before the coming of the painter, but we have sounds—as distinct from mere noise—only when the musician makes their creation. (The relation between music in the ordinary accepted meaning of the term, and the music of nature, such as the song of the birds, is almost too small to affect the argument.)

Music, in short, can be called the most universal, the most direct, and the most ideal of all the arts, and consequently, it can with some justice claim to have the least negative, if not the most positive, influence on morality, and by this we mean the bettering of man's estate, and the approximation to Aristotle's *το εὖ ζῆν* (to live well). It is more difficult for it to produce effects which are injurious, and equally difficult for the listener to mistake the meaning of the composer, and interpret it in a lower and more debased sense. If we appeal to practice and experience we find that, while some people are stirred by the grandeur of music to gird themselves and set out on some great venture or deal with the task in hand with greater energy, others regard music as a relaxation and revel in it for the love of sheer beauty. If music should fail to exalt the mind, it never succeeds in actually degrading it, but in its stead brings on a feeling of annoyance or weariness. Music can be moral and usually is; it can be unmoral, but rarely, if ever, immoral.

Music is an abstract affair in being singularly free from foreign associations and distractions; we are less disposed to have pre-conceived ideas about it, and pre-conceived ideas are not as a rule helpful. It is infinitely easier to descry vulgarity in a picture or a poem than in a sonata, and at the moment we are discussing pure and absolute music. 'The man in the street' may object to the jazz *qua* dance, but the musician may object to it *qua* music, and while the sentiments of a poem may be doubtful, its perfect technique may render it a work of art. In short, aesthetic morality is an entity quite apart from conventional standards of ordinary life, and a work of art should be judged according to the canons of art. Music, being the most abstract and the most apart, can well receive the most favourable verdict.

THE ART OF REPRESENTATION

(1925)

THE fine arts have one chief aim—the attainment of the beautiful, which will arouse aesthetic emotion. The aesthetic is an end in itself. It is a manifestation of the Life Force, the Whirl of Energy, the Spirit of Creation, call it what you will, that indefinable something that brings things into being and carries them to their appointed end. A work of art consists of a series of lines, curves, designs, colours combined in a particular way to stir our aesthetic emotion, and this can be termed rhythm. There is something intangible, non-earthly about it. Some one has said that 'the painter does not create the picture on the canvas; he merely lifts, one after another, the veils which hide it', and it is the same idea that the sculptor sets free the form imprisoned in the marble. Beauty must be at least in part objective. The artist must take his subject from this world, for he cannot delineate a void, and into this subject he must bring the supernatural element, which in its turn will create a state of ecstasy. The subject is only used as a medium, but the great danger is to make it everything. The question of Representation is fundamental.

THE ART OF REPRESENTATION

Art is suggestive, in that it deals with the truths of eternity rather than with the conventions of society. It must penetrate beneath the surface, and, for instance, in portraiture, seek to delineate the type from the individual. Exact accuracy of detail is therefore superfluous, and might even be injurious. In a landscape the whereabouts of the locality is immaterial; a certain part of a hill or field may be brown to the eye, but if all the rest be green and the general impression be one of greenness, then let the whole be thus presented to the practical exclusion of all else. Cézanne set himself out, not primarily to paint pictures, but to create forms that would express the emotions he experienced in times of inspiration, and the medium he chose was painting. The subject is used, not for its own sake, but for the sake of what the artist can set in it. The danger of extending this principle to extremes is obvious. In the cubism of Picasso and Braque, the mistake is made of eliminating the medium altogether, as far as is compatible with the restrictions imposed by a three-dimension world. Some of their creations are practically unintelligible without the title and still more with. No medium is being used capable of striking a responsive chord in the mind of the onlooker. Unless art is to be a selfish pleasure or the exquisite joy of the few, there must exist somebody to look at the picture or listen to the music or read the poem. Not that work should be produced with the audience in mind—nearly always it is the innate craving for self-expression, the artist creates simply because he feels he has to—but he must work with the possibility of there existing some one who has the same craving for expression but no technique, no opportunity or ability to transform this craving into a reality. For such people the artist must create as well as for himself. The cubist may satisfy the first of these canons of art, that it is a means of self-expression—we take his word for that—but he fails to satisfy the second and transmits nothing that is tangible. He stands alone, audacious, egotistical, a glaring challenge to the sociability of man.

Furthermore, no limitations are imposed with regard to choice of subject. Even the most ugly can be utilized and depicted, and in the hands of a master have an aesthetic significance of its own. Consequently we have the monstrosities of Jerome Bosch, the oddities of Pieter Brueghel, and the grotesqueness of the post-Impressionists. Again, the treatment of the same subject by different artists is immaterial, compared with the importance of what the artist puts into it. Look at the 'Annunciation' of Fra Lippo Lippi and that of Crivelli or of Rossetti, or compare Leonardo's Christ with that of Epstein.

Art is a thing by itself, separate from religion and ethics, and aesthetic emotion is different from sensual. Rousseau and Tolstoy never realized that the morality of a work of art is independent of the morality of the subject.

THE MUSIC OF TO-DAY

(*March* 1926)

MUSIC has been making gigantic strides during the last generation, but whether they have gone forward or backward is a matter of controversy. Some idea of what modern composers are aiming at and how they are setting about it would, however, lead to a more intelligent interest in their music.

The first important break from tradition is in the matter of harmony. Polyphonic writing, briefly speaking, implies several strands of melody (based on vocal writing), and chords 'resolving' according to rules of harmony and counterpoint, i.e. a discord must be followed, sooner or later, by a certain kind of concord. The modern writer cuts out the concord and follows one discord by another of the same or of a different kind (taking 'discords' in the technical sense as consisting of all harmonies other than the common chord and its inversions). Instead of being links in a chain, chords are accepted as independent sensations. With the adoption of new scales, new positions of chords, and new intervals, there comes a correspondingly new set of values, and all the old proportions are altered;

discords and suspensions are 'left in the air' and given a sense of finality, and key-signatures lose their significance in any scheme not based on the conventional major and minor scales.

In what might be loosely termed 'expression', music is being regarded from an entirely different angle. If a classic writer took his inspiration from, say, a waterfall or a mountain peak, or from any other aspect of nature, the emotion he felt—pleasure or fear or whatever it was—would be sublimated into a general aesthetic emotion, just as would any other kind of pleasure or fear. This would then be given musical expression. The modern writer skips the intervening stage and seeks to communicate to the listener the identical pleasure or fear that he himself experienced when looking at this particular waterfall or peak. The classicist interprets the abstract emotions roused by these phenomena in general; the modernist interprets the concrete emotions roused by these phenomena in particular. This is the basis of much of Debussy, Ravel, and other writers of the Impressionistic School. It is not a question of mere imitation but of suggestion raised to the *n*th degree. Sometimes, of course, such music, if not well written, can be far too vague and lack contact with the listener; the composer is not interpreting his emotions into sound clear enough to be significant.

Hence the inevitable reaction towards absolute music, free from all foreign associations, and of this absolutism, the French 'Six', Stravinsky, and those of the Spanish school are the chief exponents. Stress is laid on rhythm, and one can almost say that all the modern Spanish music is conceived in a medium of an orchestra of plucked instruments. Simplicity is aimed at and it becomes difficult to draw the border-line between chamber and orchestral music—a contrast to Strauss, Scriabin, and Schönberg, who indulge in enormous orchestras, elaborate scores, and complicated schemes of harmony.

PAUL DUKAS

(*July–August* 1926)

In the history of Art there have been many cases of a composer, writer, or painter achieving fame through one work, and being known subsequently only by that one work. It may be due to an early death, or to unfavourable intellectual environment, or to subservience to popular taste, or to incapacity to follow up one startling novelty with another; but usually it is due to genuine littleness of talent, and the lack of staying-power that goes with it. Repetition of success is the hall-mark of genius, the ability to say often things worth saying. The second-rate, the amateur, the dilettante concentrate all their worth into one work, and then are finished and done to the world. There are exceptions, of course—the reputations as poets of Gray and Coleridge rest on the slenderest output, while the number of known works of Giorgione can practically be counted on the fingers of one hand, but generally speaking, the rule holds good both in music and in the other arts. Charpentier, Leoncavallo, Bruch, Duparc, Boito are all 'one work' composers, and up to the present Paul Dukas has very unjustly been added to that number. *Louise*,

Pagliacci, the G minor Violin Concerto, the Seize Mélodies, *Mefistofele* are all convincing enough, but whereas other works of these writers are either non-existent or have been tried in the balance and found distinctly wanting, Dukas has never been given a fair chance. Why is it that no one, in this country at least, ever seems to have any special desire to hear anything else by the composer of that extremely brilliant and witty scherzo *L'Apprenti Sorcier*? His name figures but rarely in our concert programmes, and, as a matter of fact, some of his compositions are of the highest artistic importance.

Paul Dukas was born at Paris in 1865. Before he was twenty he had begun his studies at the Conservatoire, where he had a distinguished career, but in 1888 he only succeeded in winning the Second Prix de Rome with a cantata *Velléda*. In such competitions it is not always the best man who heads the list (did not Dvořák fail to win a prize with his *Stabat Mater*?), and this apparent rebuff only spurred Dukas on to further training, and in particular to a close study of the classics and the works of the old masters. With the collaboration of Saint-Saëns he completed the opera *Frédégonde*, which his Conservatoire teacher Guiraud had left unfinished. He worked hard at composition and his first published work, an overture to Corneille's *Polyeucte*, was performed at a Lamoureux concert in 1892. A Symphony written during 1895–6 also belongs to this 'prentice period; it is better than the overture but is too diffuse, and the thematic material is not sufficiently distinctive. This early self-discipline, so characteristic of Dukas, has had, indeed, a very marked effect on his subsequent work. It developed and intensified that keen critical faculty which has led him to publish so little, refusing with a most praiseworthy reticence to burden the world with half-evolved experiments, full of unrelated neologisms (an example that might well be followed by many of his younger contemporaries!). In the different capacities as editor of the works of Rameau and Couperin, as contributor to various reviews and periodicals, and as a professor of orchestration at the Conservatoire from 1910 to 1912 (and, at the moment, at the École Normale de Musique, Paris), he has achieved a unique reputation for erudition and sympathetic criticism. This early training, too, laid the foundation for that sound technique which allowed him in his mature work to give full play to his abundant wit and imagination, and at the same time to preserve the musical interest with significant thematic developments, harmonic progressions, and so on. It is this combination of classicism with romanticism, this application of the romantic spirit to the classical tradition, that make *L'Apprenti Sorcier* (1897) and the other outstanding works of Dukas—the Variations on a Theme of Rameau for Piano, the lyric drama *Ariane et Barbe-Bleue*, and the *Poème dansé, La Péri*—so fascinating.

A Piano Sonata in four movements, written (1899–1900) later than *L'Apprenti*, we do not place so high as the companion work for piano, the Rameau Variations. The first and fourth movements, full of interesting material, are pervaded with a restlessness now of sorrow, now of adventure, the scherzo is definitely original, but the slow movement is inclined to be diffuse. While the form and structure are eminently coherent, the Sonata seems just to lack the colour, and the light and shade that characterize the Variations. In short, the Sonata is just too classical, but for all that, it is well worth study and performance. The minor works of Dukas include a *Villanelle* for horn and piano (1906), and two piano pieces, a *Prélude élégiaque* on the name of Haydn (1909), and a contribution to the Debussy memorial number of *La Revue Musicale* (1920). Even before the war, Dukas projected a musical version of Shakespeare's

The Tempest, but so far, nothing of it has been published.

We are left then with four masterpieces, of which only one, *L'Apprenti Sorcier*, is at all well known in this country. Indeed, it is so well known and appreciated (and rightly so), that it would seem hardly necessary to recapitulate Goethe's ballad, *Der Zauberlehrling*, how there once lived a wizard with a magic broom that would do anything it was bidden on mention of a pass-word, how the apprentice took advantage of the wizard's absence to make the broom fetch water, how the apprentice forgot the other password to stop the broom, how the house was wellnigh flooded, and how the wizard arrived in the nick of time. Dukas treats the story with a verve and picturesqueness of detail, coupled with a feeling for the macabre and a mastery of orchestral effect, that make every hearing of it a continual delight. With the brilliant treatment of its themes and the excellence of its proportions, this scherzo survives the strictest of musical tests, quite apart from its literary association.

The *Variations, Interlude et Finale pour Piano, sur un thème de Rameau* (1902) are astonishingly classical in spirit without being in the least antiquarian. They could only have been written by a modern writer, but by a writer in sympathy with the traditions of the past, and it is by compositions such as this that the classics are made to live and breathe again. These variations, of which there are twelve, are all extremely free. Some discourse on points arising from different phrases of the theme, while others preserve the structure, but with practically new material. The Interlude is in the nature of a Fantasia, with brilliant cadenzas leading straight into the final twelfth variation, an extended development of the whole theme. Throughout, the counterpoint is never introduced as a display of erudition, but always forms an inherent part of the musical scheme or pattern. The whole work is thoroughly imbued with eighteenth-century clarity—how Rameau would have loved it!

Ariane et Barbe-Bleue was first produced in Paris at the Opéra Comique in 1907. The book by Maeterlinck is an entertaining version of the old legend. The first act displays a vast and sumptuous hall in Bluebeard's castle, and outside are heard the cries of the peasants proclaiming death to the tyrant. Ariane, the sixth wife, appears holding six silver keys and one golden key. She has been given permission to use the former, and with them she unlocks the six different doors that guard the treasuries of jewels, but she determines, however, to open also the seventh door, the forbidden door, with the golden key. Nothing to be seen save a black darkness, from which rises a mournful chant! Bluebeard enters and upbraids her for her disobedience, when suddenly the peasants rush in to kill him. Ariane declares he has done her no harm, and they depart in sullen silence. In the second act, Ariane has entered the forbidden chamber, and has found Bluebeard's five previous wives imprisoned there. She inspires them with courage, telling them of the wonders of the country outside, and declares she has come to set them free. With stones they break an ancient window and emerge into the light of day. In the third act they are in the hall, where they adorn themselves with the jewels from the treasuries. Suddenly, Bluebeard's return is announced. Vast noise outside. Bluebeard is fighting with the peasants, who overpower him and bring him bound into the hall. The women take pity on him and bandage his wounds. They refuse to leave Bluebeard, but Ariane says she must depart to a 'land far from here, where they still await me'.

It is a curious play, a symbolic expression of the eternal conflict of light and knowledge against darkness and ignorance, a play full of exquisite poetry of that fascinating sensuous charm of which Maeterlinck is such a master; poetry delighting in beautiful forms, beautiful figures, beautiful colours, delighting in the warmth of the sun, the song of the birds, the fragrance of the flowers, the ripple of the waves and the nectar of the air. It is sheer joy in life itself, 'when to be young was very heaven', but with this, there is coupled an element of the mysterious. There is mystery about the forbidden door and the vault which lay behind it. There is mystery about Ariane and about her mission in life. We dwell on this, because it illustrates so perfectly the mature style of Dukas. It is limpid, elastic, and, above all, intensely poetic. Dukas realizes to the full that beautiful thoughts gain by being beautifully and clearly expressed. The score of *Ariane* is a marvel of lucidity and coherence, with a curious unearthly sheen over it. The actual themes are admirably expressive, terse and to the point, and some of them are developed and transformed in the most surprising ways—especially the vivacious 'jewel' motive in the first act, with its six variants as the six doors are opened, from which pour six different cascades of jewels, from each door a different jewel, and also the grotesque Bluebeard motive with its giant-like falling intervals. The music ranges from single melodic lines, such as that of the song of the five imprisoned women, to tremendous orchestral *tuttis*, such as that in the second act, when the sunlight pours into the darkened vault, and in the distance are heard the murmurs of the sea, the sweeping of the wind through the trees, and the village clock striking the hour of midday. Throughout, the orchestration is superb, the vivid instrumental colouring changing with all the nuances of the poetry. We are not aware that *Ariane et Barbe-Bleue* has ever been staged in this country; in spite of the technical difficulties of presentation, this should be remedied as soon as possible.

The ballet *La Péri*, produced in 1912, is equally fine, but on a smaller scale. There is but one scene and two characters, the hero Iskender and the Péri, a fairy. Iskender seeks the flower of immortality, to try and recover his lost youth. At the far ends of the earth he finds Péri asleep, with a lotus flower in her hands. He takes the flower, and she awakens, frightened. The Péri is fair to look on, and to Iskender the lotus becomes like the face of desire. She dances the dance of the Péris, coming so close that sometimes her face almost touches his. He gives her back the flower, and she disappears slowly into the distance. It is a warning of his approaching end. *La Péri* is a miracle of delicate and sensuous elaboration; there are only about five themes altogether, but they are presented with wondrous and charming arabesques, delicious developments and derivatives, luscious and sparkling orchestration. The score, however, is never overloaded, the effects being gained not by reduplication of the parts (the orchestra, including twelve wood-wind and eleven brass, is by no means abnormal), but by subtle placing of the chords and the employment of suitable timbres. As in *Ariane* the music is strangely pervaded with a feeling of the magical and the supernatural.

Paul Dukas ought certainly to be better known in this country. He possesses a superb technique, both in the handling of themes, their transformations, developments, and so on, and also in the mastery over the orchestra and the knowledge of orchestral effect. There is a polish and a refinement about his style that make it never obscure, and this clarity is apparent even in the most mysterious passages of instrumental colouring. Dukas always knows what he wants to say and how to say it. He is attracted rather by subjects that savour of the weird and the unearthly, subjects that call for deep imaginative power. To some critics his themes may seem rather precious, while others may dislike his employment of the whole-tone scale, but his themes are singularly expressive in the circumstances in which they appear, while the passages or chords based on the whole-tone scale are almost invariably used for purposes of colour or of contrast. Dukas stands alone in the world of music, a strangely interesting and individual figure. He is much too fastidious to attach himself to any particular school of thought, or to fall under the influence of any particular composer. With his interest in Rameau and the classics, and his skill in giving almost every word of a symbolist play like *Ariane* its musical value, Dukas unites most successfully the sensitiveness of the romanticist with the scholarship of the musician.

AN APPRECIATION OF FORM

(1926)

Rousseau's famous dictum, that 'Mankind is born free; and everywhere he is in chains', is certainly a matter of acute controversy. Not only is it extremely questionable whether man ought to be born free (which was what Rousseau really meant), but also whether the chains of society are chains at all; whether, rather, man can only rise to complete stature of mind and of body through and by means of the society of which he is a member. The chains, if we call them that, are there, and we must make the best of them, and leave the fashioning of imaginary Utopias to the theorists. The modern economic world has no niche for the shipwrecked mariner on the desert island. This question of structure, of management, of form, is all-important in politics; in art it is no less pertinent.

It marks the difference between order and chaos. Nature is run according to formulae, from the circulation of the blood to the movements of the planets round their orbits. A language must have a grammar, and a philosopher must set his thoughts into sequence before they can become a philosophy. The ravings of a lunatic are of interest to the physiologist and the psychologist, but they seldom make good literature, any more than prize essays on the functional mandibles of the higher Lepidoptera. In the construction of a work of art, the artist must submit himself to the severest discipline. The choice of one medium, sounds—as opposed to, say, colours—and the very instruments of sound are in themselves limitations. The compass of all musical instruments, including the human voice, is not indefinite, the actual notes, too, being clearly differentiated, from the primitive pentatonic scale to the division of the octave by equal temperament into twelve intervals on the modern piano. The Western world is content with semitones, but the Eastern has recourse to quarter-tones. Further, at both extremes of the scale there are limiting frequencies, beyond which the human ear can appreciate no sounds, though scientific apparati prove that vibrations are present.

These limitations are unavoidable and inevitable. The musician must conform to them, and it serves no useful purpose trying to overstep them. The primitive who fashions portions of his altar-piece in high relief, and the ultra-realist who sets real grass, bits of wood, and other paraphernalia on a canvas side by side with colours from the brush, are as much on the wrong track as Strauss with his wind-machine in *Don Quixote* and Erik Satie with his typewriter in *Parade*. A statue will never cease to be a piece of stone or marble, however much it represents a human person (despite Pygmalion and Galatea), and a landscape will always remain a piece of canvas, however well it gives a pictorial representation of nature. An orchestra can never make the same noise as a thunder-storm, no matter how many executants are employed, but what it might do is to suggest some of the same kind of emotions as those suggested by a thunder-storm. Beethoven hit the nail on the head when he declared the Pastoral Symphony to be 'the expression of feelings rather than painting', and he might have added 'the expression of feelings in terms of music'. It is no more possible to take an abstract quality—love or hate—and establish it literally in a certain succession of sounds, than it is to set it literally on a canvas. Such is only the musical or pictorial representation of an emotional experience; it is not the emotional experience itself. The abstractness ceases and the concrete appears as soon as the medium of sounds or of colours is employed. Herein lies the fallacy of cubism and futurism, which, incidentally, Picasso has had the good sense now to realize. The medium cannot be disregarded or treated as if it were non-existent. All the movements towards realism, whether in the novel or in opera, run themselves against this brick wall at once. The stage is above all a matter of convention, and, apart from the pantomime, all realistic imitations of natural phenomena such as waterfalls, earthquakes, and the like, demand comparison with the original and suffer miserably in consequence. In fact, the qualifications 'stagey' and 'theatrical' have passed into common parlance. When the Köln Opera-house produces the 'Ring' with the assistance of the cinema and throws the waters of the Rhine and the sweeping of the clouds round Brünnhilde's fiery mountain, all on to a screen at the back of the stage, the result is undoubtedly striking and effective as a film, but as adjunct to the music, is it not too realistic? Apart from anything else, the speed of music is much slower than that of speech or action, and any attempt to co-ordinate the two is bound to meet with difficulty; one must be sacrificed for the sake of the other. Opera is the most artificial of all musical forms, and the artificiality is heightened, not only by the acting, in the literal sense of the word, by personages who, off the stage, resemble all other men and women, but also by the expression of their emotions in song, as opposed to the speech of everyday life. Though the attempt to make opera too real may be more commendable than the failure to make it real enough, yet suggestion is the basis for all art.

Suggestion, then, as opposed to imitation or reality, and this implies a medium, something tangible, whether it be a question of the instruments which produce the sound, or of the conditions—concert halls, theatres, &c.—under which the sounds are produced, or of the relationships between the sounds themselves. It is an ancient truism that there is nothing new under the sun, that any combination of sounds, lines, or words must be made from a perversion or selection of already existing sounds, lines, or words. The human mind cannot pass beyond the limits set by its three-dimension world. All the monsters of ancient mythology, the centaurs, dryads, and fauns, the deities of Egypt and Assyria with heads of one living creature and bodies of another, the Sphinxes, the Calibans, the Rimas, are syntheses of certain human and animal qualities or characteristics in unusual proximity; qualities or characteristics which existed previously, but split up among different forms of life. However freakish and modern a composition may be, the elements, the sounds and notes of which it is composed, have all been used somehow before, excepting, perhaps, in the case of instruments such as horns and trumpets, whose possibilities have been enormously increased through recent technical improvements. Revolution can be translated by Evolution, a return to first principles and a fresh start along new lines. The artist, in fact, forms part of a long tradition; he builds on the past, he uses the tools of previous artists and fashions with them his own handiwork. The genius has no time to waste thinking out new tools, he has so much to create that he accepts the spade-work done by previous generations. The second-rate makes curious and peculiar experiments to cover up the commonplace of his thought. Mr. Ernest Newman has summed the matter up: 'If musical history teaches us one thing more positively than another, it is that the works of pioneers have for posterity an antiquarian rather than an aesthetic value.' Even an inspired innovator like Debussy left the main stream of musical progress, to change the metaphor, only a little earlier on and a little higher up, but the rivulet, limpid though it was, eventually dried up and came to nothing. Palestrina, Bach, Beethoven all come on the crest of enormous waves that had been gathering themselves in the generations previous; they represent the culminating points of gradual and lengthy developments of the various art-forms of the madrigal, fugue, and sonata. Even Wagner only applied the symphonic principles to the music drama, and carried orchestration but one stage further; he always considered himself the artistic descendant of the Beethoven of the third period, the Beethoven of the Mass and the Choral Symphony.

The converse, of course, obviously does not hold true, that everything written according to the tenets of tradition is necessarily good. The product is greater than the sum-total of the parts, and the personal equation of the composer is something innate and indefinable, subject to no laws and regulations. Whence cometh inspiration we know not, but what we can know and emphasize is the enormous part that tradition plays in musical history (and in every other kind of history, for that matter). The importance of the composer having full control over his medium, and being able to express the most diverse thoughts with equal freedom, is made more pertinent by the fact, which Walter Pater pointed out in his celebrated essay on Giorgione, that in music there is the closest identification between what the composer has to say with the manner in which he says it. We have words ready to hand before the coming of the poet, and landscapes before the coming of the painter, but we have sounds—as distinct from mere noise—only when the musician makes their creation. (The relation between music in the ordinary accepted meaning of the term, and the music of nature, such as the song of the birds, is almost too small to affect the argument.) Sounds, *qua* sounds, have not the external associations of lines or words, which can have a non-aesthetical appeal to the intellect, quite apart from their place in works of art.

Finally, in a work of art there are two parties concerned—the artist and the audience. The artist does not necessarily create with the audience in mind; generally, it is his own craving for self-expression. He creates because he feels he has to, but he must work with the possibility of there existing some one with the same craving for expression, but no technique, opportunity, or ability to transform this craving into a reality. Through his medium the artist must make his work understandable to his audience. If he does not wish this, if he simply works for his own enjoyment, pleasure, or satisfaction, then he has no need to publish or exhibit. In short, the two parts of a work of art, the matter to be presented and the medium through which it is presented, the message and the expression, assume equal importance. They are interdependent and one must not predominate to the exclusion of the other. In testing any work, a double standard of criticism emerges: 'Has the composer anything to say?' and 'Does he say it well?'

The point is, that a knowledge of structure, a sense of balance and proportion, a feeling for contrasts, climaxes, and points of repose, a coherence of style, the ability to use material in the most economical and significant way, making a perfect fusion of melody, harmony, and rhythm, are the distinguishing marks of the first-rate artist as against the amateur and dilettante. Brilliancy of technique may, of course, conceal poverty of invention, and may run to seed as in some of the polyphonic monstrosities of the Netherland School, which can be made to sound the same whether played right side up or upside down, but that is not to assume that there should be no technique at all. The presence of rules and conventions, the nature of the actual forms—concerto, fugue, sonata, rondo, variation, &c.—all the contrapuntal devices—canon, inversion, augmentation, diminution, stretto, and so on—instead of hindering the artist, allow him to develop his fancy and elaborate his thought in the framework already provided him. Mr. Calvocoressi makes a succinct quotation from Mr. Clive Bell in this respect: an artistic form 'will serve the double purpose of concentrating the artist's energies and stimulating his intellect. It will be at once a canal and a goad . . . the ideal problem will be the one that raises the artist's power most while limiting his fancy least.' Some of the greatest artists of all times have worked under what seem to be the most tyrannical restrictions. The Spenserian stanza and the Shakespearian sonnet are two of the most difficult of all metrical forms. The religious convention of the pre-Renaissance painters did not prevent the introduction of contemporary portraits and familiar landscapes into their biblical subjects, nor did the absence of linear perspective lessen the delicacy of touch of the Japanese. The genius of a Bach could discern the latent possibilities in the meanest of themes, while the sketch-books of a Beethoven (models of industry!) reveal how dry bones can be clothed with forms that live and breathe and have their being. Even Mozart, the arch-formalist, could make the most exciting departures from tradition in the famous introduction to the C major String Quartet and in the operatic ending to the overture to *Don Giovanni*. Mozart, too, never seemed in the least abashed by any peculiar combination of instruments;

on the contrary, he always wrote with the most wonderful naturalness and sureness of effect whether in the two fantasies for the barrel of a musical clock or in the processional music for two flutes, five trumpets, and four drums. The freest recitative from the *St. Matthew Passion* to *Pelléas* is based on the inflexions of the human voice. The appoggiaturas of Chopin no more made him independent of a logical harmonic scheme than did the false relations of Orlando di Lasso. Ravel is always to be found in one of his most characteristic moods when looking at the past—*L'Heure Espagnole, Pavane, La Valse*—through critical modern spectacles. Scriabin evolves whole compositions from the extended use of one chord. Even in the difficult domain of programme music the only works of any value are those which can survive the strictest of musical tests, quite apart from any literary or other associations. *L'Après-midi* is revealed as an astonishingly closely-knit piece of effective writing with five clearly defined themes, while is not *Till Eulenspiegel* quite the merriest of all orchestral rondos?

Discipline, in fact, is never far absent from art, and though Beethoven affirmed that rules were meant to be broken, they can only be broken by a mature artist who knows the how and the why.

The true craftsman is never mastered by his craft; on the contrary, by means of this very discipline he himself becomes the master. *Ars est celare artem.* The eighteenth century carried convention to extremes. A Spanish king died of etiquette, and the continued spectacle of Zeus and Hera in lace and ruffles stepping through a minuet amid a shower of heroic couplets becomes as tiresome as the clichés of full- and half-close and of tonic and dominant. Our own age is by no means immune from the tyranny of consecutive thirteenths and unresolved discords, and the trouble with so many writers of to-day lies in their inability to know what to do with their new-found freedom. It turns out to be no new freedom at all, and the very insistence on avoiding a certain convention becomes in itself a new convention. On the one hand, the followers of Brahms adhering to all the framework of the classical tradition, but with no inspiration, and the result is thick, arid, pedantic; on the other hand, the followers of Debussy, dropping all shackles, and again with no inspiration, and the result is weak, flabby, invertebrate. Too much convention stifles inspiration; too little does not foster it enough. The inspiration and the convention, the message and the expression, must balance each other equally; otherwise the work of art has not achieved its object—to give the audience a vision from the artist, by which the former can lift himself from the things that are mundane, and look, even for a moment, into the infinite.

NATIONALISM IN MUSIC

(*January* 1927)

THERE is a common and highly disquietening tendency nowadays to classify composers, and indeed artists and writers generally, according to nationality, and to establish aesthetic and intellectual relationships between men whose only point in common lies in their belonging to the same political entity. True, that implies submitting to the same scheme of taxation and observing the same code of laws, but the die-hard and communist, as a rule, are not particular about acknowledging each other as fellow-citizens; and it does not need Sir Walter Raleigh's burning of his 'History of England' manuscript to convince any one that the most ordinary happening can be described differently by as many pairs of eyes as see it. Probably every schoolboy has at some time been bidden to write an essay on 'The Influence of Climate on National Character', and has duly noted all the platitudes about heat and cold and about life on the mountains as opposed to life at the sea and so on; but most platitudes have a basis of truth, and truth in small doses is not necessarily disagreeable. Certes, the climate of a country, the language and customs of the people living in it, influence very considerably the architecture, painting, and literature of that people, but affect their music to a very much smaller extent. Only bricks, made from alluvial clay, could withstand the terrific midday glare of Chaldaea and Egypt, while the Gothic church, as Emerson suggested, 'originated in a rude adaptation of the forest trees with all their boughs to a festal or solemn arcade', and the sky-scraper is the direct outcome of modern economic competition. The sombre skies of the Netherlands, the blue skies of Italy, the dazzling skies of Spain, inevitably created 'schools', each with its own peculiar atmosphere; and as regards landscape, the painter takes what he sees about him. Crivelli's 'Annunciation', Veronese's 'Surrender of the Children of Darius', and Tiepolo's 'Finding of Moses' illustrate for us different phases of Venetian life and manners. The Shield of Achilles, the Tragedy of Paolo and Francesca, the Roguery of Falstaff, the Sorrows of Werther: are they not all immortal transcriptions of contemporary experiences? The writer is further limited, not only by the niceties of the language in which he writes, but also by the very sounds of that language, and at once guttural German or liquid Italian can alter the character of an essay or sonnet.

Music, on the other hand, is infinitely more self-sufficing and independent. It can be heard and appreciated, given adequate conditions of performance, at the same time by different audiences all over the world; while translations of printed and copies of painted works never repeat the wonder of the originals. Music is in all probability, too, the earliest art evolved by the savage, being a development and elaboration into singing and dancing of cries of everyday life and movements expressive of ordinary emotions. Though national instruments and national dances may orient, technically, the early musical development of a people along certain lines, yet folk-songs have remarkable affinities. The emotions they express are general and fundamental, while the most cursory study of comparative mythology emphasizes the similarity of the primitive mind, for instance, in seeking to explain the mysteries of the world in terms of natural phenomena. There even exists the possibility of one basic musical scale common to mankind from China to Peru, the pentatonic; and a folk-tune can suffer different appearances under circumstantially the same form, whether due to parallel indigenous growth or to assimilation from one people to another. (The music in Chopin's nocturne *Les Soupirs* heard by the composer on the Mediterranean coast also occurs in the piano introduction to one of Mrs. Kennedy-Fraser's *Songs of the Hebrides*, volume i.) Finally, music is quite the most absolute of the arts. Sounds, apart from mere noise, only come into being at the will of the musician, and must be judged entirely on their own merit, so to speak; but a line of poetry, made up of words open to anybody's use in ordinary discussion, must make material sense as well as stir our aesthetic emotion.

Music, then, by its very nature, is not so much international—for that would imply a synthesis of things national—as non-national. It has really nothing to do with creeds, religions, politics, or boundaries. Bach and Beethoven could write Masses for Roman Catholic ritual; Debussy could capture the spirit of Andalusia in *Une Soirée dans Grenade*; Berlioz, the most patriotic of Frenchmen, had no illusions about the musical bankruptcy of Paris under the Bourbon Restoration—his heroes were Shakespeare and Gluck, and his greatest personal triumphs were gained in Russia; while Wagner, from what we know now, was in all probability a Jew (the son of the actor Geyer), which lends a singular piquancy to all his scurrilous anti-Semitic pamphleteering! In fact, the less national a composer is, the better. Nations are often distinguished from each other more by their points of weakness than by their points of strength. There are people in Britain, France, Germany, and Italy who are both brave, witty, learned, and cultured; but in Britain there is a larger proportion of respectability, in France of finicalness, in Germany of sentimental *Wehmut*, and in Italy of full-throatedness, than in any other country. As soon as music—meaning that of a civilized (horrid word!) people—becomes exclusively national, it is in danger of becoming respectable, or finicking, or sentimental, or full-throated. There is but one stream of musical progress whose source is tradition and whose energy is inspiration; and to this stream all endeavours must join before they can become permanent or significant. Any new art must be 'fertilized', to adopt an expression of Mr. Ernest Newman, by the old before it can flower forth in all its majesty and power. It was precisely on this very point that the Russian 'Five' came to grief. By declaiming Russia for the Russians and transfiguring the moujik into an Apollo, they isolated their art instead of fertilizing it, and sterility was the inevitable result. When they studied a classic quartet or sonata, they would plunge into the development section with the remark 'and now for the mathematics'. Borodin, it is true, did see the folly of relying entirely on the folk-tunes to carry him through and produced those magnificent pieces of symphonic development, the Symphony in B minor and the *Prince Igor* Dances; but, generally speaking, 'repetition' of themes instead of 'development' has been the curse of Russian music from Serov to Stravinsky. Originality of melody and brightness of colour certainly go far, but not far enough to make up for the absence of contrapuntal structure and form.

We do not deny that folk-songs can have a powerful animating influence, but like whole-tone scales, exotic timbres, and experiments in harmony, they must be used only as means to an end and not made ends in themselves. Folk-songs are characterized normally by sincerity and virility, and these are qualities present in the works of composers such as Vaughan Williams, Sibelius, and de Falla, who choose not to quote folk-music note by note, but to write *in the idiom of* folk-music. The material is so assimilated as to become the very flesh and blood of the composer. With the 'London' Symphony and the 'Kalevala' Tone-poems the listener is first concerned, not with the chimes of Westminster or the wilds of Finland, but with magnificent stretches of sheer abstract music. In the dances from *El Amor Brujo* and

The Three-cornered Hat Manuel de Falla sublimates to the level of works of art the guitar-twanging and vocal lines of gipsy Spain, just as Chopin sublimated the mazurkas and polonaises of Poland. Abstractness and sublimation: let these be the methods whereby programme music (disputable term!) and music based on folk-songs can be identified with that huge main stream.

Insist on the concrete, and *Finlandia* turns into a tourist handbook; insist on the realistic, and *Hugh the Drover* develops into an historical essay. Nationalism in music is an excellent servant but an overbearing master. Great national events or experiences have not been productive of great works of music, and the *Kaisermarsch*, the *1812 Overture*, *Carillon*, are mere *pièces d'occasion*, differing only in degree and not in kind from *The Battle of Prague* and *The Siege of Delhi*. 'Give me the songs of a people, and I care not who make their laws'—quite; provided one knows what to do with the songs; provided one strips them of the outside dressing and reveals the humanity beneath; provided one uses them to create works of art, non-national and universal.

ARCHITECTURE OR COLOUR?

(*September* 1927)

THERE is probably no subject in music on which so much has been written as that of Romanticism, but it reaches down to fundamentals and consequently remains perennially fresh. Most writers[1] are now agreed on the undesirability of sharply differentiating between things classical and things romantic; there is a misleading chronological flavour about these terms—classical composers belonging more to the eighteenth century and romantic composers more to the nineteenth—whereas it is not a question of centuries but of states of mind. A work of art can be analysed into content and form, thought and expression, two parts that fuse together into a whole that is so immeasurably greater than the sum-total of the parts. Leaving out of account the unfathomable question of why and how some mortals are peculiarly gifted with the power of creating and composing, how is the process of creation achieved, and how come these parts of a work of art to be so fused? In the embryo stage, does the will to create

[1] Cf. 'The Fusion of Classicism and Romanticism', Mrs. Frank Liebich (*Musical Times*, April 1927).

solve the problem of presentation, or does the problem of presentation stimulate the will to create? In the finished product, which is the dominant characteristic, which the recessive? This would appear to be the point at issue.

There are some composers who seem to stress content, who are concerned with ideas (in the abstract), and who experience emotions to which they desire to give expression. Some medium has to be chosen—it may be music, philosophy, science—in fact any medium will suffice, for the concept partakes of the universal and not of the particular. There are present almost unlimited potentialities of expression, but (almost paradoxically) once the mind has fixed on music, it concentrates on it to the utter exclusion of all else, and only music can possibly be associated with it. There are other composers who seem to stress form, who are intensely interested in the possibilities of their medium, music, and who desire to cultivate it as beautifully as they can. They are musicians by instinct, seeking for the concept to accord with the form; they compose because they cannot help it, but, again paradoxically, the mind originally concerned with the particular enlarges to the universal, and occupies itself too, with values other than those purely musical—literary, artistic, and so forth. Here then are two types of composers: to the former belong Bach, Beethoven, Elgar; to the latter, Mozart, Wagner, Debussy. Beethoven, for example, has often been compared to Michael Angelo almost on the assumption that if suggestion or other influence had been brought to play on the ante-natal mind, Beethoven might have decorated a Sistine Chapel and Michael Angelo might have written a Choral Symphony. Again, Mozart has been likened to Watteau, but the impression is inevitable that no amount of ante-natal or other suggestion would have influenced their minds from their predestined occupations; their work runs on parallel lines that never meet. It is Beethoven the *thinker* who is apparent, but Mozart the *musician*.

So with the music itself. Some music is concerned primarily with shapes, masses, contrasts, and little emphasis is laid on the medium through which it is presented. Bach used arias and melodies many times over in entirely different contexts. Of his extant fourteen Clavier Concertos only four were originally written as such. The famous D minor, for example, started as a Violin Concerto, while later the composer arranged it for the organ with additional wind parts in the orchestra, setting, further, this arrangement of the slow movement as an accompaniment to an independent four-part chorus in a cantata! Not only can instrumentation vary, but also *tempo*. Elgar transforms the C minor Fugue into a riotous carnival; Schweitzer interprets it as an elegiac threnody. Handel made previous use of many of *The Messiah* airs in distinctly secular surroundings. The version for two pianofortes of Brahms's *Haydn Variations* and F minor Quintet are as interesting and important as the so-called 'originals'. Stravinsky makes *Pétrouchka* almost as vital for two hands on the pianoforte as for the orchestra of eighty or a hundred. Music of this sort is complete in itself, has no leanings towards the other arts, is 'abstract' in the literal sense of the word; it is architectural in its balance and proportion.

On the other hand, there are composers, occupied with lines, contours, nuances, who take a form—string quartet, opera, symphony—and endeavour to fill this form with the most appropriate and exquisite sound. This sound is conceived only in terms of its setting and presentation. Mozart's music is not interchangeable, but with impeccable taste he knew exactly how to differentiate between the trio for pianoforte, clarinet, and viola, the concerto for flute and harp (two instruments which he detested), the fantasias for musical clock, and the processional music for two flutes, five trumpets, and four drums. Liszt boasted that he could perform effectively on the pianoforte (actual instrumentation excluded) anything from the classical orchestral repertoire, whereupon Mendelssohn inquired if he could play the opening bars of Mozart's G minor Symphony—a passage scored for strings alone, incapable of any transliteration whatever! Berlioz, too, had an uncanny flair for timbre, for giving to instruments passages uniquely and inevitably suited to their own peculiar qualities. Wagner's *Leit-motif* transformations and developments acquire their vital significance through the orchestra. What would the *Ring* be without the bass clarinet, or *Tristan* without the cor anglais? Works such as Ravel's Quartet or Septet lose their *raison d'être* if played on any other combination. Colour (despite its dangerous associations of orchestral fireworks and theosophist speculations) would appear to be the only satisfactory term to cover adequately the meaning, and by this there is implied not the identification of a particular colour with a particular sound or tonality, but rather the subtle interplay of lights and shadows. Colour must be wooed and loved for its own sake, and not merely used as a servant, to be summoned and dismissed at will.

Here, then, are composers divided generally into architecturalists and colourists, and here the seeming paradox resolves itself. The music of the architecturalist can stand alone and aloof, and requires no reference to or assistance from associations not absolutely contained in the music. The music of the colourist, on the other hand, requires intense exactness in presentation, and welcomes associations—literary and pictorial—in so far as they can contribute to this exactness. While, as we have seen, Bach transfers movements from one cantata to another, Mozart never fails to distinguish between the dramatis personae in his operas, and songs (and, still less, overtures) cannot possibly be changed from one work to another. While Beethoven was comparatively little sensitive to the significance of words—witness *Fidelio* and the Scottish Songs—Debussy turned deliberately for his texts to the Symbolists and *les Décadents*. Picasso and Derain, in *The Three-cornered Hat* and *La Boutique Fantasque*, have openly allied themselves with de Falla and Rossini. Beethoven detested being asked what his music meant, but Scriabin had to plunge into the intricacies of theosophy in explanation of *Prometheus*.

Many musicians, too—Berlioz, Wagner, Schumann, Saint-Saëns, Cyril Scott, and others—have changed the pen of the composer for that of the author (with varying degrees of success, to be sure!), and musical criticism has assumed a new value and import in assessing the *mot juste* and determining whether the composer has or has not given the most complete and epigrammatic turn to a phrase or melody. The more recent art-forms that have been cultivated—*genre* music, the symphonic poem, the music drama, the ballet—lean towards a union with other arts, and not towards an isolation of the music (despite the reaction now in favour of the small orchestra and the *concerto grosso* of the eighteenth century). The wider education of modern composers, the more prominent part they take in the body politic, and the technical improvements in the construction of musical instruments, are all pertinent, without doubt, but do not explain everything. As was said above, it is a question not of centuries, but of states of mind. The painters Cézanne and Monet offer almost an exact instance. The former occupied himself with synthesis, the latter with analysis; the former was interested in the ensemble, the latter in the details. Cézanne declared that 'il n'y a pas de lignes, il n'y a pas de modèle, il n'y a que des contrastes', and Monet that 'le personnage principal d'un tableau, c'est la lumière'.

ARCHITECTURE OR COLOUR?

Of course no division, theoretical or chronological, can be absolutely conclusive, and, in a sense, the qualities of neither architecture nor colour can ever be wholly absent from a work of art. A sense of form and a feeling for expression must both be manifest, otherwise the music remains lifeless and inert. Further, universality is the distinguishing feature of genius; it is only a question whether the particular proceeds from the universal, or whether the universal is reached from the particular. It depends from what standpoint the composer views his art. The spiritual realist achieves beauty almost in spite of music; the inspired craftsman (not technician) achieves beauty almost because of music. Who is bold enough to say that one is better than the other?

MANUEL DE FALLA

(*December* 1927)

IT has often been remarked that the music of Spain has had to be written by foreigners (from Glinka to Lord Berners!), and indeed, the creation of a *Fantasie espagnole* came almost to be regarded as a masterpiece whereby the budding apprentice in orchestration could enter into full membership of the craft. Though happily the reproach has now little meaning, yet the Spaniards themselves have been partly to blame, and, ironically enough, the artist perhaps most representative of their national culture and tradition, they called, not El Español—but El Greco! Spain is as rich as any other country in the matter of folk-lore, national songs, and the dance, but though the common people have ever been jealous of their inheritance, it must ruefully be confessed that no outstanding personality in music, except Vittoria, was produced until the latter part of the nineteenth century. Felipe Pedrell, as composer, savant, and teacher, gave the preliminary urge to modern Spanish musical thought, which gathered strength with Albeniz, Granados, and Turina, and revealed the powerful and penetrating mind of de Falla.

MANUEL DE FALLA

Manuel de Falla was born at Cadiz in 1876, and at an early age began his musical studies at home. At the Madrid Conservatoire he studied piano with Tragó and composition with Pedrell. His early compositions include operettas and theatre music, written as often as not under financial pressure, but some chamber music was performed with success, though none of it has been published. The year 1905 marked a turning-point. De Falla won a prize for piano-playing (though mere virtuosity has never attracted him), and the *Academia de Bellas Artes* crowned his opera, *La Vida Breve*, a remarkable work already full of characteristic rhythm and vitality. The drama of Fernandez Shaw is a simple Andalusian tale of unrequited love, treated with a simplicity that amounts to grandeur.

From 1907 to 1914 de Falla lived in Paris, where he received welcome and encouragement from Debussy, Dukas, and other composers. In spite of material hardships and the at times uninspiring occupation of music-teaching, it is during this period that the ideas germinated that found expression in his later mature work. Some compositions of a limpid grace and charm—a suite of *Quatre pièces espagnoles* for the piano (*Aragonesa, Cubana, Montañesa, Andaluza*), and a set of *Trois Mélodies* of Théophile Gautier (*Les Colombes,*

Chinoiserie, Séguedille)—were published, while *La Vida Breve* received its first performance at Nice in 1913. At the outbreak of the war, de Falla returned to Spain, settling in Granada, and published *Siete Canciones Españolas* ('Seven Popular Spanish Songs'), of which the *Jota* is the best known. The Nocturnes, *Noches en los jardines de España* ('Nights in the Gardens of Spain'), symphonic impressions for piano and orchestra, were finished in 1915. This is true symphonic music with pairs of contrasting themes, combinations, augmentations, and diminutions, in a web of delightful arabesques at once clear and elusive. The first Nocturne, 'perfumed, starlit, mysterious', is set among the flower-laden terraces of the Generalife at Granada, and the suppressed excitement of the second, *Danse lointaine*, reaches full expression only in the third, *Dans les jardins de la Sierra de Cordoue* (Cordova), which breaks into tango rhythm just before the close.

The ballet with songs, *El Amor Brujo* ('Love the Magician'), is a gipsy tale, belonging to the *género chico*, a typically Spanish form of dramatic art—short essays in genre, eclectic in style and treatment, interspersed with songs and dancing. *El Amor Brujo* (1915), the book by Martinez Sierra, tells how the evil spirit of a dead man interposes between two earthly lovers, but perishes in the end, conquered by love. *El Sombrero de tres picos* ('The Three-cornered Hat'), represented now by the Russian Ballet continuously since 1919, is almost too well known to require description. Curiously enough, this brilliant comedy of P. A. de Alarcon, adapted on this occasion by Martinez Sierra, with the miller and his pretty wife and the old roué of a governor, forms the subject of the only opera completed by Hugo Wolf (*Der Corregidor*). Both ballets belong to Andalusia.

In some ways the most important work of de Falla is the puppet opera *El Retablo de Maese Pedro* ('Master Peter's Puppet Show'), first performed in 1923. With *Pelléas et Mélisande*, *Savitri*, and *Doktor Faust*, it lays down the gauntlet to Wagnerian idealization and Italian naturalism, and refuses to submit to the tyranny of the grand manner and the old tradition. The composer has taken the episode described in Chapter 26, Part II, of *Don Quixote*, where the hero witnesses the performance by puppets of the old 'romance' of Don Gayferos and his lady, Melisendra, who has been captured by the Moors. The showman's boy explains the action as it proceeds, but Don Quixote, taking the tragedy in real earnest, breaks up the puppet stage, and in an address to the spectators, extols the profession of knight-errantry. The Concerto (recalling the *concerto grosso* of the eighteenth century) for harpsichord, flute, oboe, clarinet, violin, and violoncello is a later work in three movements, austere, subtle.

Other works are the *Fantasia Baetica* for piano (1919), a rhapsodical affair with a lyrical intermezzo; the *Homenaje* for guitar (1921), written for the Debussy memorial number of *La Revue Musicale*; *Psyché*, a poem of G. Jean-Aubry set for voice, flute, harp, violin, viola, and violoncello (1927); *A Córdoba*, a sonnet of Góngora, set for voice and harp.

De Falla is eminently a national composer, though his sparse output would seem to belie it. The Spanish genius has ever been generous and profuse in the matter of creative work, and lacking rather in the critical faculty. While Lope de Vega is credited with over 2,000 plays and Albeniz with over 200 opus-numbers, de Falla with deliberate fastidiousness and self-discipline has kept back much that he has written, and has refrained from publication till the work in question has been submitted to all possible criticism and care. The Nocturnes, for example, were begun in Paris years before his return to Spain, and *El Sombrero* received its first performance in a shorter and much less elaborate form two years before the Russian Ballet took it up (it is, of course, the revision which has been published). Moreover, de Falla's style, retaining its spontaneity, is terse and vital to a degree. He holds in abhorrence, in his own words, 'academical routine, false rhetoric, obsolete formulae', and his compositions have showed a steady progress towards elimination and simplification. His first opera is a full-dress affair, but the two ballets and the puppet opera are on the scale of one-act performances. The drift has been, too, from the full orchestra of *La Vida Breve* and *El Sombrero*, to the chamber orchestras of *El Amor Brujo* and *El Retablo*, and the chamber music of the Concerto and *Psyché*. It is an orchestration, picturesque, which depends for effect, not on masses of sound, but on subtle spacing of chords and contrasts of timbres; incidentally, it relies considerably on the wind, and frequently employs a piano (in *El Retablo*, a harpsichord, instead). The themes, too, are vivid and to the point, and are made to yield the fullest expression that is in them (as for instance in the first part of the pantomime in *El Amor Brujo*, and in the proclamation from *El Retablo*); perhaps those of the later works, especially of the Concerto, are more condensed and concentrated, but de Falla is far too much of a stylist to lapse into monotony or obscurity. Economy of material does not necessarily imply lack of inspiration.

Spain is a land of sharp lines and contrasts. The brilliant sunshine casts lights and shadows that dominate all Spanish painting from Zurbaran to Zuloaga; miserable hovels and filthy slums cluster round a wondrous cathedral heavy with precious stones; the language is epigrammatic, for the Spaniard dearly loves a proverb; passions swiftly change from love to hate and from hate to love, while death is conceived in terms of life and life in terms of death. A directness of vision led Columbus to discover America, Torquemada to erect an *auto-da-fé* at Toledo, and Cervantes to write the first novel. An insistence on reality can result in the naturalism of the national sport, in the ecstasy of a St. Teresa, and in what the writer, 'Azorin', described as 'the eternal poetry of everyday things'. And de Falla, as has been said, is deeply Spanish. His clear-cut melodies, almost exaggerated by Picasso in *El Sombrero*, the quasi-coloraturas of *La Vida Breve*, the ornamentation of the Nocturnes, the roulades and fanfares of *El Retablo*, allow of no smudging. While there is a certain stridency about the Fantasia, and the Concerto is conceived in a spirit of rare contemplation, an exquisite sensibility distinguishes the *Récit du Pêcheur*, the grief of the miller's wife, and Melisendra in her tower. With a wholly peculiar reticence, however, the composer never lets his gaiety descend to the common or his mysticism rise to the passionate—both a strength and a weakness. Still, de Falla's style is characteristically dynamic and markedly rhythmic, reaching its most obvious and at the same time its most grateful expression in the *Danse rituelle du feu*, and the Farruca (Dance of the Miller). The technique of the piano Fantasia (not such a successful work as some of his others), for instance, exploits largely the percussion qualities of the instrument, and in the Concerto the composer abandons the piano for the less emotional but not unexpressive harpsichord. It is, in fact, a style conceived in a medium of plucked instruments, especially guitars; a style that seeks to evoke the music of Spain, not actually by quoting it, but by writing in the spirit of it, whether evoking the music of the gipsies (*La Vida Breve*), Moorish music (*El Amor Brujo*), the music of old-time chivalry (*El Retablo*), or religious music (the Concerto).

Spain, however, is not one country but several, not one kingdom but many, and racial differences are ever rising to the surface. De Falla, by birth, upbringing, residence, and mental outlook, belongs to Andalusia—the land of the joyous and pleasure-loving, whose life is a perpetual dance of colour and sunshine; the land of the Alhambra at Granada, of the Mosque at Cordova, of the Giralda and Alcazar at Seville, with their traceries, fantasies, and decorations; Andalusia, the stronghold of the Moors in Spain, the meeting-place of East and West! This is peculiarly significant, for despite de Falla's firm hold on tonality, there are constant melodic undulations and turns of phrase that reveal an oriental or quasi-oriental influence. With the important exception of *El Retablo* (and possibly also of the Concerto), all de Falla's larger works, both in subject and treatment, breathe the spirit of Andalusia; the *Homenaje* makes a graceful quotation from Debussy's *Une Soirée dans Grenade*; but the exhilarating score of *El Sombrero*, with its moments of sadness, pulsates most with the light and laughter of the southern sierras. It is the pride of Castille that finds pathetic expression in *El Retablo*.

And so we have a composer brought up in the enthusiasm of the Spanish musical renaissance, developing under the generous sympathy of the modern French school, but always remaining intensely national, and elevating popular rhythms and vocal lines into audacious and piquant works of art. De Falla's work reacts against the turgid romanticism of the nineteenth century, and reverts to the clarity of the eighteenth-century clavecinistes; the dry flavour of the guitar gives it movement, the song of the people gives it life. His almost angular drawing (recalling in some ways that of El Greco, though he lacks the hysteria that led the latter to distort so much) depicts, now a jota danced in some shady patio, now a tiny splash of water on a moonlit terrace; now a monk, now a Moor; now the pomp and circumstance of a Spain that is past, now the healthy vitality of a Spain that is alive. Above all, there is the personality behind the drawing—a personality scholarly, human, critical, sympathetic.

MUSIC AND THE MODERN WORLD

(*December* 1928)

It is an interesting theme for speculation whether Life should imitate Art (as Oscar Wilde suggested), or whether Art should hold the mirror up to Nature. Does the artist exist in spite of and in defiance of his age, or is he the product and result of it? Does he lead the way, or does he but summarize contemporary thought? Is he a pioneer or a popular hero?

In either case there is a very near bond between an artist and his environment, a bond that is both intellectual and economic. Rousseau's dictum that 'Mankind is born free; and everywhere he is in chains' is a matter of acute controversy. Not only is it extremely questionable whether man ought to be born free (which was what Rousseau really meant), but also whether the chains of society are chains at all; whether, rather, man can only rise to complete stature of mind and body through and by means of the society of which he is a member. The hermit can never rid his subconscious mind of early and childhood impressions, and, moreover, in his person, represents the sum-total of generations of gradual and lengthy development, a development both mental and physical, which Samuel Butler has described at length in his own queer and picturesque way. Palestrina, Bach, Beethoven appeared at the culminating points in the history of the madrigal, fugue, and sonata, while Wagner only applied the symphonic principles to the music-drama and carried orchestration but one stage further. The idea that the artist is a being set aside from his fellow men is a dangerous half-truth. Moreover, he is much more influenced by economic conditions than is at first supposed, and the activities of the composer, for example, tend to be limited by the exigencies of performance. He is generally human enough to want to hear his own work himself, and he will not consistently choose a medium or write in a grade of difficulty incompatible with what his time and place have to offer. The madrigalists produced a profusion of airs and ballets in an age when the ability to sing a part in a madrigal was esteemed as much a part of ordinary culture and breeding as the capacity to take a hand at bridge in the present day. The eighteenth century, an age of individual aristocratic patronage and small rococo palaces, witnessed the rise of that singularly intimate branch of music, the string quartet. Would Haydn have been so prolific a composer if he had not had the Esterhazy court band at his immediate disposal for rehearsal of his symphonies? Was not the appearance of a Diaghileff inevitable in a country where the ballet had for long been appreciated as an independent art-form? Did not the monstrous orchestras of Strauss and Mahler but reflect the feeling for the colossal, which permeated imperial Germany?

There have been three features characteristic of the history of the modern world (and especially of the world during the last decade) which have had powerful and stimulating influences on art and music. First, there has been a very general shifting of political power and importance from aristocracies (though, to be sure, there still remain aristocracies of brains and culture) to democracies (or rather to autocracies, for the mob-mind seeks not to lead but to follow). National sympathies are aroused (and not infrequently exaggerated), appeal is constantly being made to the rights of small nations, and 'self-determination' becomes the catchword of the day. This awakening race-consciousness, though still rather helpless, has led to a more real and thorough understanding of folk-music. We have probably heard the last of the Scottish rhapsodies written by Germans, Spanish fantasias by Russians, Oriental suites by Englishmen. The elegant cosmopolitanism of these guides to foreign lands gives place to a zealous preservation by nationals of their own native art. Bloch, Sibelius, Janáček, have spoken for their people in racial accents proud and unashamed. Béla Bartók, Vaughan Williams, de Falla, have, with scrupulous scholarship, collected, arranged and utilized the folk-music of their respective countries. Liszt might have done it, had he been less of a showman and more of an artist, but the real pioneers in this work were the Russian 'Five', unless we include the Elizabethan writers for the virginals. Then, it was exceptional; now, it is the rule.

Further, there has been a much wider diffusion of capital and wealth, resulting from the breakdown of the three great European empires, the gradual disappearance of the privileged classes, the taxation of landed property, and the cheapening of luxuries such as the motor-car. The days of the munificent patron seem to be numbered, as painters have the good sense to realize when they apply their art to poster-work and advertising. The constitutional statesman relying on a parliamentary majority is not so inclined to spend public money on the fine arts as the enlightened despot such as a Medicis or a Ludwig of Bavaria, and we find now that opera-houses and orchestral organizations are almost everywhere passing through severe financial crises. Which is perhaps a reason why contemporary composers tend to fight shy of large symphonic and dramatic productions, and to turn their attention more to the smaller art-forms and to works for chamber orchestra—works both easier and less expensive to perform. Music for the masses finds its expression, for better or for worse, in community singing, in cheaper editions of the classics, in the publication of a flood of instruction and introductory manuals to catch the young and tempt the uninitiated, in cinema music (finding its nadir in the cinema organ), and in a wholesale distribution of mechanical instruments, gramophones, pianolas, wireless sets, and so forth. (There has been but little music written originally and directly for the cinema; Mascagni and Hindemith have tried their hand at it without much success, Strauss made himself rather ridiculous with the film version of *Der Rosenkavalier*, while the Russian Ballet experimented with the cinema in *Ode*. Hindemith has composed music specially for the pianola, and also for the mechanical organ.)

This is certainly a mechanical age, and the overwhelming part played by machinery is the second great feature of our modern life. Machines race everywhere, burrow under the earth, swim under water, and fly in the air. Labour-saving devices are poured out in mass-production. Wires, chimney-stalks, cranes, railway lines make fantastic and bizarre angles and shadows between heaven and earth. The ether becomes a huge telephone exchange, and space and time are playthings in the hands of children. Aesthetically, the significance of this is twofold: a sense of terrific power under control, and a cult of the straight line rather than that of the curve. The cubism of a Picasso or a Braque is a direct translation on a two-dimension canvas. Verhaeren and Carl Sandburg photograph the smoke and steel of London and Chicago. Limitation of space, fighting with gigantic needs, forces the sky-scraper upward; elsewhere, a Stockholm town hall and a Leipzig railway station are modern solutions of the problem. In music the effect is no less pertinent, and especially in the work of Stravinsky. 'Through him', remarks Mr. Rosenberg in *Musical Portraits*, 'music has become again cubical, lapidary, massive, mechanistic. . . . Contours are become grim, severe, angular. Melodies are sharp, rigid, asymmetrical. Chords are uncouth, square clusters of notes. . . . Above all, there is rhythm, rhythm rectangular and sheer and emphatic, rhythm that lunges and beats and reiterates and dances with all the steely perfect tirelessness of the machine.' The relentless repetitions and maddening throbbing of mighty engines reverberate through *Le Sacre,* the *Symphonies d'instruments à vent* (to be played *without expression*) have all the immobility of a façade of iron and steel, while *Pétrouchka* is an epic of puppets and wires. Debussy can be metallic in the early A minor Prélude, in *Masques,* in *Mouvement,* and the *Fugal Overture* of Holst resounds with blows from a hammer. Honegger mounts the footplate of *Pacific 231*, and the gruesome mechanistic paraphernalia of modern war are exposed in *The Planets* of Holst, *Ein Heldenleben* of Strauss, and *Pagine di Guerra* of Casella. Prokofieff, very successfully, makes an even more precise attempt to portray this terrific power and these angular lines in the factory engines of *Le Pas d'Acier.* Machinery can move in a pathetic adagio, or it can speed like a brilliant scherzo. Can there not be beauty of line in a cruiser as well as in a frigate, in a limousine as in a four-in-hand? Late twentieth-century music is certainly dynamic. The dry, biting tones of the wind-band predominate over the suavities of the strings, the percussion have become an orchestra with a technique of their own, and the sweeping pedal-effects of a Liszt are replaced by the brisk staccato of a Percy Grainger.

This terrific power implies speed as well as strength, and new dimensions and proportions are at once created, just as distances have to be revised beside the modern means of locomotion. Symphonic longueurs and romantic outpourings are now frankly *demodé*, the cultivation of the *genre* is very characteristic, and a terseness of style is almost universal. The solo concerto, the four-movement symphony, the three-act opera are all much shorter, or else metamorphosed into something such as the concerto grosso, or the suite for chamber orchestra or the ballet, with quite different foci, climaxes, and points of interest. The actual texture, too, of the music is drawn infinitely tighter and closer. Resolutions of discords are assumed and not expressed, final chords are left 'in the air', while harmonies on different planes are sounded simultaneously, instead of leading one to the other. As Rococo was the age of the arabesque, so now economy of material is the order of the day, and the evolution of this species of 'short hand' renders music elliptic and epigrammatic. Many examples can be drawn from Holst, Goossens, Ravel, in short from most contemporary composers.

The third powerful influence on modern music has been that of the dance, and the modern dance is characterized by jazz—an insistence on syncopation, reinforced by a liberal use of percussion; syncopation, that is to say, exploited not as a means to the general effect, but as an end in itself. Syncopation, as a source of interest, has of course always been at the disposal of the composer, and the romanticists, for example, made abundant use of it. From the very beginning, too, the dance has had an enormous influence on music, and, in fact, music may be said to have evolved direct from two constituent elements, the song and the dance. Further, composers have always interested themselves in contemporary dances; the Elizabethans transcribed them for the virginals; the Suites and Partitas of Bach consist of sets of allemandes, courantes, gavottes, gigues, and the like; the minuet won a place in the classical symphony; and the waltz has had such illustrious admirers and exponents as Schubert, Chopin, Brahms, and Ravel. The twentieth-century composer sets himself then a legitimate problem in trying to vitalize the clichés and formulas of jazz, and we have the Ragtimes of Stravinsky, the Tangos of Milhaud, the Blues of Ravel; the Dance Suites of Hindemith and Toch; the *Rhapsody in Blue* of Gershwin, *Jonny spielt auf?* of Křenek; the 'Voice-band' of Burian. Are these experiments in sublimation effective, convincing, permanent? Or has the concert hall merely been turned into a *dancing*, and the theatre into a cabaret?

The cult of real folk-song, the power of machinery, the rhythm of jazz are not, of course, the only influences bearing on modern music, nor are they the only component parts into which it can be analysed, and, further, composers such as Elgar, Rachmaninoff, Puccini seem to belong apart to different traditions. Rather is it that in these points the modern social, industrial, and economic world impinges directly and leaves definite imprint on the world of music. But is the first quarter of the twentieth century the dusk of the old world or the dawn of the new?

THE EGYPTIAN HELEN

(*December* 1928)

It is interesting to speculate on the great characters of drama and fiction and to follow them beyond what the poet and writer have told us. Occasionally it has been done, and sometimes by the author himself, who has a lingering affection for the creatures of his imagination (witness *The Three Musketeers, Sherlock Holmes,* and *The Forsyte Saga*). St. John Ervine pays a visit to Belmont after the nuptials of Portia and Bassanio; Gordon Bottomley recounts the early story of the daughters of King Lear; and various works of Dickens have been continued by his admirers. *Il Barbiere* and *La Nozze di Figaro* are but two chapters in the intriguing history of Figaro and the Count; *Elektra* carries on the tragedy of the *Oresteia*; Carmencita is the daughter of Carmen, and Lohengrin the son of Parsifal. It would be amusing, too, to know some of the further experiences of Edie Ochiltree, or of Rebecca, Lady Crawley, or of Gianni Schicchi. What did Nekhlyudov do with his life after Maslova had refused him in Siberia? Did Eliza really marry the vapid Freddy and not the redoubtable Professor

Higgins? How did Walther find Eva after all the pother she gave him in winning her? Then there are the historical mysteries, Pope Joan, The Man in the Iron Mask, Louis XVII, and so forth—always fertile subjects for investigation.

The case of Helen of Troy is one of the most fascinating of all these problems. Her name has become a byword for that peerless beauty that sends warriors to arms and inspires poets to song, and it is for ever coupled with one of the most celebrated wars in history, a war which led to the writing of two of the world's great epics. If the Trojan War had never happened, it would have been necessary to have invented it to provide a stage on which those famous characters—Odysseus, Menelaus, Ajax, Agamemnon, Cassandra, Helen, and the rest—might act, live, and have their being. (Perhaps the war *was* invented. But one cannot enter upon the niceties of historical scholarship at the moment.) The most prominent are Odysseus and Helen, and something is certainly known about the former, his life in Ithaca, his stratagems at Troy, his wanderings round about the Aegean and the Black Sea (Scylla and Charybdis may reasonably have been situated at the Dardanelles), and his eventual return to his faithful Penelope, after sending the suitors about their own business.

Tradition has it, too, that home life began to weary and to pall; that he set out again on his voyages; that on his return he found his home burnt down by pirates, his wife captured, his servants killed, and desolation everywhere; that then he betook himself to Egypt, on hearing of the existence there of a strange and mysterious being, a reincarnation of the Helen, the most beautiful woman in the world; that he had further adventures in Egypt, all of which furnished Andrew Lang and Rider Haggard with material for very readable romances.

Helen is, in many respects, a much more shadowy figure than Odysseus, and one is naturally curious to know what Menelaus, the injured husband, thought of his erring spouse, whether Helen was glad to return to him after her hectic existence with Paris; what was their attitude to each other after Troy had fallen, and whether their feelings towards each other had changed. This is the theme chosen by Hofmannsthal and Strauss in their latest opera *Die ägyptische Helena*, which received its *première* at Dresden in the spring of this year and which has now been performed in Vienna and Berlin. It is the sixth opera created by this remarkable collaboration of a practical opera conductor and orchestral composer, with a symbolist poet and mystic philosopher. The former relying on experience, the latter on intuition; the one, of the world, the other, outside it. Their reactions to each other can be traced in a most interesting volume of correspondence published a year or two ago, and now available in an English translation.

In the first act of *Die ägyptische Helena* Menelaus has resolved to offer Helen as an atonement for her share in the Trojan War, and is about to slay her on the boat as they pass the isle of the goddess Aithra, a favourite of the sea-god, Poseidon. Aithra prevents this by raising a storm which shipwrecks the boat on the isle, and Menelaus and Helen enter the palace of Aithra, who now bids her elfs and spirits imitate the Trojan battle-cry. Menelaus dashes out once more to fight Paris, whose voice he seems to hear, while Aithra gives a potion of forgetfulness to Helen, and takes her away to rest. When Menelaus returns, Aithra tells him that the woman he brought away from Troy was a phantom, and, after pouring out to him also a draught of forgetfulness, explains that the real Helen was hidden for ten years by the gods in Egypt. Aithra reveals her here, clad in brilliant raiment, and Menelaus is carried away by the deception. The pair are wafted to a lonely palm-grove at the foot of Mount Atlas, where the scene of the second act is laid. The magic, however, has not been altogether successful. Menelaus is now convinced that on Aithra's isle he slew the real Helen (in that imaginary fight with the Trojans), and that the present Helen is but an illusion, while Helen is determined to win back wholly the love of her husband. A desert chieftain, Altair, comes as Aithra's vassal to greet them, but while Menelaus is invited to go hunting, Altair, dazzled by her beauty, begs Helen to fly away with him. Helen, summoning Aithra's help, offers her husband a potion to cancel the effects of the previous one, and Menelaus is made to realize that the being before him is the actual, real, guilty Helen. A dangerous plan, but it succeeds. Menelaus raises his dagger, but falls at her feet lost in love and admiration. Their child Hermione is brought to them over the desert in the chariot of Poseidon, and they depart back to Sparta, united and happy.

The opera is a mixture of good and bad. The idea of the play is excellent, and one feels that anything might happen when one approaches the mysterious, inscrutable land of Egypt, but the plot was all more or less worked out in the first act. Why repeat the process in a different setting? The alternate separations and conciliations of Menelaus and Helen are confusing, while the episode of

Altair and still more that of the hunt add little, if anything, to the argument.

The music has, certainly, spectacular moments —the whirling wood-wind figure associated with the distraught mind of Menelaus, the storm in the middle and the terzetto at the end of the first act, the hunt music in the second act; while the various transformation scenes—Helen awakening from her ten years' sleep and revealed to the admiring Menelaus, or the horses of Poseidon charging over the desert—suggest to the composer all manner of possibilities in gorgeous *tuttis*. Strauss's command over the orchestra is still as complete as ever, and the sensuous quality of colour is exploited as of old; but, as a whole, the opera is frankly not up to standard. There are too many of these diatonic excursions with chromatics superimposed on tonic and dominant, leading up to a six-four climax, all of which are apt to sound so *démodé* nowadays. The Oriental exoticism at the appearance of Altair fails to impress, and the themes, generally, have not the mark of distinction. The work is theatrical, not dramatic. Further, there are passages which sound ominously derivative, whether from *Ariadne auf Naxos* or *Der Rosenkavalier*, or, worse still, from *Der Ring des Nibelungen*. In fact, it savours too much of a revue: music by Strauss and

Wagner, scenery by Selfridge, wigs by Clarkson, cigarettes by Abdulla. All of which is a pity. *Die ägyptische Helena* makes a tolerable evening's amusement, but from Strauss we expect more than that. He is now sixty-four years of age; is it too late?

OPERA SINCE WAGNER

(*April* 1929)

OPERA is passing through a time of crisis. The underlying principles are being re-examined, conventional standards revised, and new criteria of values applied. Meanwhile, the difficulties of performance are more acute than ever.

The construction of the older opera-houses is illuminating. Stalls fill the area, while boxes rise tier upon tier, leaving a restricted and ill-arranged gallery for the common herd. But with the passing of political power from aristocracies, and the wider diffusion of learning, opera has ceased to be an appanage of one class. The stage caters now for a new public without the old traditions but also without the old prejudices; and this period of transition, with all its serious financial complications, is certainly difficult. It is indeed astonishing that opera should continue to be written at all.

It has three great rivals—programme music, the ballet, and the dramatic oratorio. The symphonic poem lets the imagination of the hearer run free by dispensing with all awkward scenic representations, and by not distracting his attention with heroes and heroines who can sing the parts but cannot look or act them. The great battles round and about the symphonic poem were waged in the nineteenth century, and a stormy but fascinating chapter in the history of music was, in all probability, closed with Strauss's *Alpine Symphony* in 1915.

The ballet, as evolved by Diaghileff, is a production of the twentieth century. It concentrates on the stage performers, making them things of joy and beauty. The difficulty of the combination of actor and singer is surmounted by relying only on the actor and substituting gesture and mime for the human voice, while a Picasso or a Derain is called on for the scenery. Interest in the ballet has passed rather from the Russians to the French. In *Apollo Musagetes*, Stravinsky has not repeated his early successes which he abandoned in favour of experimentation and wanderings in the wilderness, but the French 'Six', with the exception of Milhaud, have consistently used the ballet in preference to the opera. What is called the 'dramatic oratorio' is a still more recent development or revival. Stage conventions are abandoned; and the plastic material and objective feeling offered by a chorus (as opposed to solo voices which have more individuality and consequently must remain more subjective) have led to Stravinsky's *Œdipus Rex* and Honegger's *Roi David*.

The ballet and the oratorio are important phenomena of this post-Wagnerian epoch and of our reaction against the superb gestures and monstrous emotionalism of the super-men, heroes, and libertines of the Romantic movement. No longer do composers lay bare their grief-stricken souls in public, and no longer do the gods of Valhalla sit in judgement in the realm of the aesthetic. Contemporary art is at once more reserved and more human; and it is along these two lines that post-Wagnerian operatic history has proceeded.

Modern opera seeks to establish a closer intimacy between the stage and the audience. The stage is made to reflect contemporary modes and manners, and the audience sees itself as others see it. The celestial beings of Gluck, the *haute noblesse* of Mozart, Verdi's lords and ladies, Wagner's gods and monsters—these no longer supply the librettist with his material; and the modern democratic world turns rather to *Boris Godounov*—that passionate outcry of the common people against tyranny and oppression.

The early reactions against the supremacy of Bayreuth found expression in three different styles. The Italian triumvirate, Mascagni, Leoncavallo, Puccini, made opera brutally realistic and peopled the stage with the flesh and blood of their own time—an example followed by Wolf-Ferrari with *I Giojelli della Madonna,* Charpentier with *Louise,* and Eugen d'Albert with *Tiefland.* (The events in *Pagliacci* actually happened in real life, and Leoncavallo's father, a judge on circuit, had to try the case.) Humperdinck, on the other hand, turned to the fairy tale, but *Hänsel und Gretel* remained a solitary success, unless we include *Ariane et Barbe-Bleue* by Dukas, which more properly belongs to the tradition re-established in *Pelléas et Mélisande* and derived from *Boris.* In this, the third pronounced anti-Wagnerian force, the vocal line is plastic, closely following the natural inflexions of the spoken voice; and economy used both in material and treatment.

This is the first stage in the search for something more reserved and more human, but it is still what may be called the Wagnerian period, which Strauss carried practically to its finale with *Der Rosenkavalier.* Pfitzner's *Palestrina* and Schillings's *Mona Lisa* form a kind of coda, while Schreker grafted on to the Bayreuth stock the eroticism and problem drama of the decade just before the War.

Then came the Great War, with its breaking down of traditions, loosening of controls, and parcelling out of intellects into groups with boundaries, both natural and unnatural. The post-

Wagnerian epoch of chaos and experiment was ushered in. Not that nothing of permanent interest and value has been composed during the last ten or fifteen years; but no outstanding personality has appeared with the genius and influence capable of succeeding to the supreme position held by Wagner in his time.

It is possible, however, to distinguish up to a point between the different forms assumed by modern opera, and the different points of view taken up by operatic composers. The most prominent tendency is to emphasize or at least not to conceal the conventions. Scenery is no longer made to give as plausible an imitation as possible of woods and rivers, storms and sunsets, but to suggest them. Exact verisimilitude is obviously impossible, so why attempt it at all? The stage, from being elaborately realistic, becomes now expressionistically simple, while the music tends to revert to the old formal divisions of aria, duet, pantomime, concerted finale, and so forth, and spoken dialogue is once again admitted. Strauss experimented thus in *Ariadne auf Naxos*, but returned to the 'grand manner' in *Die Frau ohne Schatten*. Both of Ravel's operas, *L'Heure Espagnole* and *L'Enfant et les Sortilèges*, can be divided into set 'numbers', the latter being indeed a kind of ballet-opera with its musette, American waltz, fox-trot between the tea-pot and the tea-cup, aria for coloratura soprano, fugal finale, and so forth. *Hugh the Drover* is styled by Vaughan Williams a ballad-opera, and Stravinsky's *Mavra* is an opera-buffa, while Hindemith packed *Cardillac* with the inventions, fugues, passacaglias, and all the polyphony of the *concerto grosso*.

Two further developments have arisen from this concentration of material. Carry the intimacy of the theatre a stage farther, and the result is the chamber opera, in which the singers can be counted on the fingers of one hand, and the orchestra consists of a few solo instrumentalists—thus Holst's *Savitri*, Stravinsky's *L'Histoire du Soldat*, Hindemith's *Hin und Zurück*. Carry the conventionalizing of the characters a stage farther, and turn them into puppets. Busoni's *Arlecchino* is descended from the Italian *commedia dell' arte*, and his *Doktor Faust* from the old popular puppet-play, centuries older than Goethe. *Das Nusch-Nuschi* by Hindemith is entitled 'a play for Burmese marionettes', and de Falla's *El Retablo de Maese Pedro* is to be performed by puppets, with the singing heard 'off'.

This process of simplification characterizes much contemporary music—the texture is drawn tighter, and the actions and workings-out are made more terse. The race in big orchestras has meanwhile come to an end, while the melodic lines and harmonic strands are sharper and more concentrated.

The other main line of operatic development results from the nationalist spirit in music. Folklore and national legends are drawn upon; and many composers base their styles on their country's folk-songs, not actually by quoting them but by assimilating their spirit and reproducing it anew in modern conditions. This nationalism is largely a heritage from the Russian 'Five', and it tends to manifest itself most in those countries which are now enjoying a renaissance of music; in Britain with Rutland Boughton's *Immortal Hour*, Holst's *At the Boar's Head*; in Spain with *Les Goyescas* by Granados, de Falla's *La Vida Breve*; in Hungary with Bartók's *Bluebeard's Castle*; in Czechoslovakia with *Jenufa* by Janáček.

The step from nationalism to internationalism is logical. Křenek's *Jonny spielt auf* is cosmopolitan to a degree; it presses into service the motor-car, the radio, and the film, while the music is largely based on fox-trot rhythms. The scene is laid now by the side of an Alpine glacier, now in the lounge of a West-end hotel, now in a railway terminus.

Approximation to the revue and the cabaret is carried farther by Kurt Weill, Burian, Grosz, and other central European opera composers.

Contemporary methods and modes of expression, whether of the simple villager or the sophisticated dweller in the town, have, then, affected modern opera considerably. Finally, there are the works which refuse to be classified, such as Holst's *Perfect Fool*, the parody of opera, coming appropriately from the land of 'Punch'; the lyrical *Village Romeo and Juliet* of Delius; Prokofieff's satiric *Love of the Three Oranges*; Ethel Smyth's humorous *Boatswain's Mate*; Alban Berg's passionate *Wozzeck*. Such are some of the modern contributions to what is perhaps the most artificial and most controversial of all the art-forms in music, the opera.

PAUL HINDEMITH

(*April* 1929)

It is notorious that in the matter of artistic outlook, a generation is apt to react most violently against that immediately preceding and to revert to earlier ideals and perceptions. The pendulum swings swiftly from one extreme to the other. John Donne and Jane Austen are now at the height of their influence, Tennyson and the pre-Raphaelites are counted old-fashioned, and the days of the Yellow Book seem deliriously remote. In the other arts the process is somewhat similar. In the 'nineties the music-drama and the leit-motif reigned supreme, but most of the younger composers of to-day (of those, that is to say, who have arrived at full maturity since the war) quite definitely turn to Bach as their master guide and not to Wagner and the Romantics. The eighteenth century witnessed the rise to adult stature of the art of music, and development during the nineteenth century was largely oriented along two main lines. First, in point of chronology, the *Lied*, from Schubert to Hugo Wolf, assumed importance as an independent art-form and came to be introduced into instrumental music—as in the symphonies of Brahms and Bruckner, where many of the most significant movements are lyrical rather than strictly symphonic. Second, the actual texture of music, as in *Tristan*, was enormously elaborated, and harmony came to be conceived, largely by the French Impressionists, vertically rather than horizontally. The first expansion is that of melody, the second that of harmony, and now the twentieth century in its turn interests itself vastly in the resources of counterpoint—though, to be sure, a work of art is an indissoluble whole, that is so much greater than the sum-total of the parts. All that is implied is that, at the moment, one aspect of music is receiving perhaps closer attention and investigation than the others; Bach never experimented in chords like the early Florentines, and Wagner occupied himself more with harmonic subtleties than with rhythmic possibilities. This new occupation with the methods of polyphony implies, naturally, the use of polyphonic art-forms such as the fugue, toccata, passacaglia, basso ostinato, where the interest is primarily contrapuntal, revolving round one theme or phrase and exploiting all its latent possibilities; and it implies the abandonment of the sonata form, where the interest is aroused primarily by the clash and interplay of two contrasting themes or sets of contrasting harmonies. The appeal is made to the intellect rather than to the emotions; orgies of sound and rhapsodic outbursts as ends in themselves are strongly disavowed; the warmth and sentiment usually associated with Romanticism are regarded with suspicion and disfavour; in short, it is music that is strongly abstract and definitely objective. The most distinguished member and leader (certainly as far as Germany is concerned) of this group of young polyphonists is Paul Hindemith. It is true that before the war Reger was turning out fugues, unaccompanied instrumental sonatas, suites, concerti grossi, and so forth by the dozen, but he never reached the spirit of Bach and Handel, only the letter. He was never able to rid himself either of the thickness of texture so characteristic of his time (reaching its height in the works of Franz Schreker and the middle period of Strauss), or of his own curious combination of *Sehnsucht* and *Schwärmerei.* The music of Bach and Hindemith is terse, and is not sentimental—not that the latter composer is a pale academic imitator of the former; far from it, and herein lies the peculiar and important contribution of Hindemith to contemporary musical history. To the free melodic line and elaborate harmonic schemes sanctioned and evolved by modern practice, he applies all the firm logic of keen contrapuntal thought.

Hindemith was born in November 1895 at Hanau am Main. He began his music studies at an early age, and later worked under Arnold Mendelssohn at Darmstadt, and under Bernard Sekles at the Conservatoire at Frankfurt am Main. He led the orchestra in the Frankfurt opera-house from 1915 until 1923, when the Amar Quartet came into being, largely a creation of Hindemith, who had now become a virtuoso on the viola (the instrument he plays in the Quartet). Meanwhile from 1921 he had directed the chamber music festivals at Donaueschingen (transferred in 1927 to Baden-Baden), festivals devoted to modern music, at which many of his own compositions and also important works by Milhaud, Toch, Křenek, von Webern, and others have been performed. In 1927 Hindemith was appointed Professor of Composition at the Berlin Conservatoire. He is a prolific composer, but has withheld from publication many works, even though they may have been dignified with opus numbers. His first publication consisted of *Drei Stücke*, for 'cello and piano, Op. 8 (1917), and his second of the First String Quartet, Op. 10 (1919), but maturity of expression really only began with the Third String Quartet, Op. 22

(1922), and ripened with the song-cycle *Das Marienleben*, Op. 27 (1924).

The published works from Op. 10 to Op. 21 inclusive comprise two string quartets, three one-act operas, a group of short sonatas for stringed instruments, a volume of songs, and a dance-suite for piano. The string quartets, Op. 10 in F minor and Op. 16 in C major, contain some excellent writing, and the mastery over the medium is very evident. Both the quartets have powerful first movements, and expressive slow movements, but the finales err on the side of length. The slow movement (theme and variations) of Op. 10 and the first movement of Op. 16 with its rich set of four subjects are specially well-knit and developed, and the themes, generally, are admirably plastic (a characteristic of practically all Hindemith's work), capable of withstanding all the varied handling they receive. The, at times, intense chromaticism, however, betokens the friend of Tristan, and Hindemith's first opera, *Mörder, Hoffnung der Frauen*, Op. 12, a mysterious symbolic affair (text by Oscar Kokoschka), is quite frankly a music-drama; indeed, one of the principal themes would seem to have come straight from the garden of King Mark's castle, and uncouth gigantic figures from the land of the Nibelungs stalk gloomily and brood over the deep.

Sancta Susanna, Op. 21 (text by August Stramm), is a much terser work, despite the rather erotic nature of the subject, that of a nun who feels the call of the outside world. The music is almost entirely evolved from one far-flung chromatic melody heard at the beginning, and the full orchestra is used but sparingly, some of the effects (a storm portrayed by three flutes) being astonishingly direct. There are only three solo singing parts, and the chorus is only used for brief moments. *Das Nusch-Nuschi*, Op. 20 (entitled *Ein Spiel für burmanische Marionetten* by the playwright, Franz Blei), breaks away from symphonic development of chromatic themes and reverts to the formal divisions of aria and dance, the melodic line being free but at the same time firm. The work is a kind of satiric comedy, and the element of the grotesque (cleverly exploited by Hindemith in other works) enters with the fantastic rattle of xylophones. Hindemith, indeed, already more or less abandoned the creation of elaborate harmonic complexities, and developed his style into something more sharply rhythmic in the group of sonatas comprised in Op. 11 (two for violin and piano, one for 'cello and piano, one for viola and piano, and one for unaccompanied viola), composed variously from 1920 to 1923.

But the new ground has to be explored, and hints of whole-tones, Impressionist harmony, sonatina form, neo-Handelian melodies flit across the pages, though Hindemith, always the skilled technician, never commits the solecism (unlike some of his contemporaries) of mixing styles and making clashing effects which neither please nor attract, but only offend. The works in Op. 11 are transitional, but are eminently playable (especially the short Violin Sonata in E flat, though the viola sonatas are perhaps more typical) by executants who wish to extend their repertory, but are not prepared to associate themselves unduly with all the eccentricities that are apt to pass as modern music. The *Tanzstücke* for piano, Op. 19, attack the problem of rhythm from its most approachable side, that of the dance (in this case, the modern dance), while a compromise is aimed at in the Eight Songs for Soprano, Op. 18 (to poems by various contemporary writers); the atmosphere of the individual poems is preserved by the most direct and economical rhythmic means, repetition of accompanying figures, and the like. All these early works, though perhaps immature, reveal, on the part of the composer, a most remarkable command over his material, whether sonata or music-drama, whether for unaccompanied instrumental solo or for full orchestra—the Second String Quartet is particularly masterly; and they are further distinguished by the gradual predominance of rhythmic over harmonic expression, and by the gradual transmutation of tonal into formal values.

This simpler harmonic texture, with hints of atonality and adumbrated with rhythmic audacities, characterizes the works from Op. 22 to Op. 26 inclusive. With the extremely original and daring Third String Quartet, Op. 22, Hindemith definitely discards sonata form as the basis for instrumental composition, and, further, ceases to attach key-signatures to his works. This string quartet is brief and terse, though in five movements; the first movement is a free fugue rising swiftly to a big climax; the second is founded on fierce rhythmic effects mostly in unison, and the third on a swinging melody (but to be played *mit wenig Ausdruck*) mostly to pizzicato accompaniments; the fourth is a wild fantasia, and the fifth a curious rondo. The other compositions written about this time, anticipate. In the two works which comprise Op. 24, the composer uses what is to become his favourite medium, the concerto (*Konzert*), referring not, of course, to the strange virtuosic monstrosity of the nineteenth century, but to the *concerto grosso* of the century previous. The movements in these concerti are several, and the orchestra is not only limited in size, but the leadership passes from the strings to the wind. The chamber-music, Op. 24, No. 1, is written for a chamber orchestra (the finale being a species of fox-trot), and Op. 24, No. 2, for five instruments (flute, oboe, clarinet, bassoon, and horn). The themes, though firm and largely modelled for the dance, are free, and the composer makes use of them, fanciful, satiric, bizarre. The same ironic qualities are found in the Suite for Piano, Op. 26, entitled *1922*. The fifth and last number (a ragtime) of this suite bears attached to it a most interesting confession of faith, '. . . Play this piece wildly, but always in very strict time, like a machine. Consider the piano here as an interesting kind of instrument of percussion. . . .' (*Spiele dieses Stück sehr wild, aber stets sehr stramm im Rhythmus, wie eine Maschine. Betrachte hier das Klavier als eine interessante Art Schlagzeug.*) This use of the percussive rather than the expressional qualities of the instrument is, of course, characteristic of much modern music, and Hindemith, later, carries it to its logical conclusion by dispensing with the variable personal equation of the performer and composing directly for the mechanistic pianola. This process of condensation and concentration can be traced, too, in the two unaccompanied sonatas included in Op. 25 (for viola and 'cello respectively), and in *Die Junge Magd*, Op. 23 (to poems by Georg Trakl), for alto, flute, clarinet, and string quartet.

The latter work in style and composition foreshadows the song-cycle, *Das Marienleben*, Op. 27, a setting of fifteen poems of Rainer Maria Rilke for soprano and piano. Here Hindemith applies all his skill of polyphonic writing and appreciation of concerto form to the song-cycle; the second song is conceived as a passacaglia, the ninth as a fugato, the thirteenth as a basso ostinato, the fourteenth as a theme and variations (the bass of the theme being of equal importance with the theme itself); the fifth resembles in miniature the first movement of a concerto, and the eighth finishes with a basso ostinato. Frequently the structure is composed of three voices (one sung by the soprano and two by the piano) related to each other on a strictly polyphonic basis. Recitatives alternate with firm counterpoint, and sonorities are obtained by the severest and simplest means. The calm mysticism of the poems is further intensified by the introduction of a modal atmosphere and feeling (rather than of actual archaic modal writing and of anything savouring of the pseudo-antique, which disfigures, for example, so much of the work of the pre-Raphaelites).

The themes are open and plastic, but are firmly and surely kneaded together. Though conventional key-signatures are not employed, yet the sense of tonality, however free, is always retained, and a fundamental note is never lost sight of or forgotten. Finally, rhythm is conceived not as an end in itself, but arises naturally out of the wealth of polyphonic writing. (From the very beginning, however, Hindemith's favourite indication and direction over his music has been *fliessend.*) We dwell on *Das Marienleben*, as it contains so many qualities and characteristics typical of Hindemith's later period, the principal works of which are a string quartet, a string trio, eight concerti for various combinations of instruments (with or without solo parts), two operas, and a volume of piano music. The Fourth String Quartet, Op. 32, and the Trio, Op. 34, both date from 1924, and have four movements; the former consists of a fugue, a slow movement, a *Kleine Marsch* (*vivace*), and a passacaglia (with twenty-seven versions of the theme, ending with a fugato); the latter of a toccata, a short slow movement, a short scherzo (mostly *pizzicato*), and a fugue. All the movements are, in short, built round one central theme, but the treatment of the fugue is interesting. The first movement of the Quartet begins with the fugal exposition, first of the principal, then of the second subject, followed by development of both in fugal wise, by a cadenza, by further development, and ending with a strict and complete recapitulation of the exposition of the first subject. In the Trio, the fugue consists of a terse but full exposition and development of the principal subject in duple rhythm, a short but complicated exposition of the second (full of intricacies and subtleties in *tempo*), a fugal development of both in triple rhythm, a pedal point of chords in sevenths in the highest octave of the violin while the viola and 'cello expound both subjects in free canon, leading to a restatement of the first subject in unison and a powerful cadence.

Of the four concerti grouped in Op. 36 (composed variously from 1924 to 1927), the most brilliant, indeed one of the most brilliant works that Hindemith has as yet produced, is No. 3 (1925) for solo violin and large chamber orchestra of twenty-four (but including no violins). The first movement, entitled 'Signal' (in which the violin does not enter), is original and dramatic; rushing semiquavers and a strict rhythmic figure accompany a daring fanfare on the cornet, and lead to the allegro proper, founded on three themes each with masterly independent developments; the third movement is a *Nachtstück* (one of Hindemith's favourite forms); the fourth is definitely fugal, but there are episodes for the violin accompanied by the drums, in this case light jazz drums; and there is a short, rapid, ghostly finale. The Concerto, Op. 36, No. 1, for obbligato piano and twelve solo instruments (five wood-wind, three brass, four strings), is a curious work, the writing for the piano being almost entirely in two single parts, one for each hand, somewhat in the style of a Bach Invention. This treatment suits exactly the grotesque and bizarre third movement—*Kleines Potpourri*, but the absence of full rich piano tone makes itself felt, especially in the slow movement. The first and fourth movements are each cleverly built up on one theme or figure enunciated at the beginning. The first movement of the Concerto, Op. 36, No. 2, for obbligato 'cello and ten solo instruments (four wood-wind, three brass, three strings) is a toccata, and the finale a gavotte, both brief and effective, but the middle movements are rather long drawn-out. The same tendency is to be found in the Concerto, Op. 36, No. 4, for solo viola and chamber orchestra (twenty-two players in all, but excluding violins and violas), though the slow movement works up, thoughtful and ruminating, to a fine climax, and the finale, some ten variations on a military march with a solo cadenza in the middle, is a brilliant affair. Two further solo concerti comprise Op. 46: No. 1 for viola d'amore, No. 2 for organ, both with chamber orchestra. The orchestra of the former resembles that of the viola concerto in excluding violins and violas, but otherwise it is smaller; the viola d'amore, however, is hardly an instrument with a loud enough tone to withstand four movements of modern contrapuntal technique.

The instrumentation of these concerti is noteworthy for the not uncommon absence of the upper strings, and for the employment together of trumpet, horn, and trombone, either singly (as in the piano, 'cello, viola d'amore works) or in pairs; the trumpet, sometimes muted, frequently assumes very special prominence and importance. A Concerto for Full Orchestra, Op. 38 (1925), is almost a contradiction in terms, but Hindemith manages to achieve concentration by alternating *tuttis* with three extended trios of solo violin, oboe, and bassoon in the first movement, by turning the third movement into a march for wood-wind alone, and by confining the finale to the limits of a basso ostinato. There is some very skilful writing both in this work and in the Concert-music for Wind Instruments, Op. 41 (1927), in which the composer tries to sublimate into art-forms the music of the military band and the café orchestra, one of the movements being a most ingenious set of six variations and fugato on the folk-tune, 'Prinz Eugen'. Considering the normal colours of Hindemith's orchestral palette, the composition of such a work as this is both logical and natural. These eight concerti (mostly in four movements) are, taken as a whole, remarkably terse and closely wrought, though single movements can be too drawn-out. The most powerful rhythms come to be sustained by the vitality of the themes, but there are times when the themes seem to be stretched out on a most uncomfortable Procrustean bed to fit the technical exigencies of the moment. Melodies, in fact, are apt to be considered only for the possibilities they offer for contrapuntal treatment, and the quality of the thematic material consequently suffers. In most cases, Hindemith guards against these dangers successfully, but here and there one feels that the music is ceasing to be intellectual and is becoming merely cerebral.

The opera *Cardillac*, Op. 39 (1926), in three acts and four scenes, represents, perhaps, the most complete expression of Hindemith's polyphonic style. The text has been adapted by Ferdinand Lion from Hoffmann's story, *Das Fräulein von Scuderi*, and the action is set in seventeenth-century

Paris. Cardillac is the name of the famous goldsmith who fashions works of exquisite beauty, but his customers, as if afflicted by a strange curse, always come to be murdered and robbed of the jewels. An officer, in love with Cardillac's daughter, determines to buy a necklace and solve the mystery. Cardillac tries to dissuade him, and the daughter begins to have an inkling of the truth. An attempt is made, unsuccessfully, on the life of the officer, who now realizes that the murderer has been Cardillac himself; the goldsmith cannot bear to separate himself from the works of art he has created. Cardillac, now thoroughly unpopular on account of all the misfortunes associated with his work, is threatened by the populace, and confesses; whereat he is set upon with fury and dies. *Cardillac* is certainly a most interesting contribution to a very controversial subject. First, it is not a music drama, but an opera; it is in set 'numbers', aria, duet, pantomime, and so forth (the contemporary revivals, especially in Germany, of the stage works of Handel, Mozart, and early Verdi, assume peculiar significance in this respect); there is a chamber orchestra of some forty players, who are largely treated as soloists, various 'numbers' being orchestrated only for certain groups of instruments, while the saxophone has a prominent position in the score; the work begins and ends with massive choral writing, and the love-duet is conspicuous by its absence. Finally, Hindemith turns the opera into a huge concerto. The first act is in the nature of the exposition of the problem, the second of the development, the third of the resolution. In the second scene of the first act, we see one of the actual murders being committed; a cavalier goes to visit a lady, at her request, with a necklace bought from Cardillac, and a masked figure follows him, plunges a dagger in his back, secures the jewel and disappears. The musical treatment of this scene is indeed curious; the ardent wooing of the cavalier (in pantomime, not song) is accompanied by an Invention for two flutes on an ostinato of the strings with other wind entering later, while the appearance of the masked figure is heralded with complete silence. The closing chorus in the third act, when the populace wrest the truth from the goldsmith, is an elaborate passacaglia; the big duet in the second act between Cardillac and his daughter is a fugato, the orchestra supplying the other 'voices'. This return to purely formal principles is, without a doubt, an unusual method to sustain the dramatic interest in a work, especially when a psychological figure such as Cardillac occupies the stage, but the experiment is worth most careful examination, though imitation by less experienced and less qualified technicians would certainly be most dangerous.

The chamber opera, *Hin und zurück*, Op. 45 (text by Marcellus Schiffer), is a most engaging trifle. The performance lasts but a few minutes, there are five singing roles, and the orchestra consists of flute, clarinet, saxophone, bassoon, trumpet, trombone, and two pianos (one for four hands, the other for two), while the climax of the work, a monologue for a ghostly figure who appears through a trapdoor, is set for harmonium. *Hin und zurück* consists of a prelude, aria, duet, and trio, leading to the monologue, followed by the previous trio, duet, and aria, but with all the stage action and the musical phrases in reverse order. It is a domestic tragedy of jealousy, culminating in the shooting of the woman and suicide of the man. Then the mysterious figure appears, expounds life and death as part of a cycle, and suggests that to the powers above it makes little difference whether man is born and dies, or dies and is born again. In the two sets of piano music comprising Op. 37, there is much intense, uncompromising writing, full of rhythmic intricacies, now in canon and imitation, now in cadenza. The style is percussive, though polyphonic, while the cadenza is restored (as also in much of the chamber music) to its rightful place as a piece of far-flung rhythm or of free fantasy, instead of merely being a vehicle for virtuosic display. In some respects, however, Hindemith's piano music is not really pianistic (just as *Cardillac* is not really grateful to the singer), the composer being more interested in the thought than in the expression, in the linear form than in the medium used. Other later works are *Der Dämon*, Op. 28, a dance-pantomime, set for a chamber orchestra of ten, and recalling, rather, the Stravinsky of the *Sacre* period; two sonatas for unaccompanied violin, and one for two flutes in canon, comprising Op. 31, where concentration is achieved through strict economy of phrasing; *Liederbuch für a capella Chor*, Op. 33, a revival of an old form; *Die Serenaden*, Op. 35, for soprano, oboe, viola, and 'cello, an intimate and personal work; *Tutti-fäntchen*, a Christmas fairy-tale in song and dance.

It is no mere coincidence that the music of the most prominent of Germany's younger composers should be architectural in form, when it is precisely in architecture that Germany is specializing and experimenting more than any other country of Europe. A new living style of building rises to meet the contemporary demand for railway stations, factories, hospitals, picture-houses, and so forth, while the profuse and elaborate decorations of the empire period are replaced, both in outward structures and indoor furnishings, by the simplicity of line of the republic. The German architect of to-day is not afraid to experiment on a large scale, trying to satisfy the new economic needs according to artistic standards. The mentality of Hindemith is similarly quite definitely of the present and not of the past; he follows the events and happenings of the world about him, and makes use of contemporary methods of thought and expression, but never drifts into a mere mouthpiece for his generation—his personal equation is too strong. Though he is a brilliant technician, yet he is saved from pedantry by his sense of humour, finding expression often in the satiric or the grotesque. He revives the concerto, creates it anew, and applies it to the song-cycle and the opera; he experiments with different combinations of solo instruments, and, latterly, abandons the full orchestra as uneconomic and unsuitable; he works with new forms such as the chamber opera; he sublimates the marches of the military band into an art-form; he plays with the rhythms of fox-trots; he sets to music the poetry of the *avant-garde*. But Hindemith goes further in his attempt to coordinate life and art, to bring art down to the level of life and to raise life to the level of art. He writes for mechanical instruments, and Op. 40 comprises a toccata for pianola and a suite for mechanical organ; he composes music also for mechanical organ, Op. 42, to accompany the film, *Felix the Cat*; he interests himself in the youthful music enthusiasts, with his Op. 43—instrumental and choral music, but more especially with the *Schulwerk*, Op. 44—several sets of pieces, some for two violins, others for three violins, others for string quartet, others for string orchestra, all to be played in the first position; finally he is concerned about the disappearance of the amateur, and Op. 45, *Sing- und Spielmusiken für Liebhaber und Musikfreunde*, sets of choral and instrumental music, is prefaced with the remark that this music is intended neither for the concert-hall nor for the artist, but is to be performed by intimate circles of music-lovers in their own homes. Hindemith is certainly a prolific composer, but this does not end the total of his activities. He has been leader of an orchestra, member of a string quartet, solo virtuoso; he is both propagandist and professor of the 'new music'; he writes critical essays and he draws sketches in black and white. And he is only thirty-three years old.

SERGE PROKOFIEFF

(*April–May* 1929)

THE life of an artist can sometimes be used to illustrate his work. The biography of Prokofieff is comparatively uneventful, as such things go, but the circumstances of it happen to be peculiarly significant. He was born in 1891 in the former Russian government of Jekaterinoslav, began his music lessons at an early age at home, and then studied under Glière and Taneieff at Moscow. He was alarmingly precocious. He began to compose at the age of five, and wrote his first opera when eight years old; two or three years later came a symphony and an opera in four acts. In 1904 he was sent to the Conservatoire in St. Petersburg, where he studied piano under Anette Essipoff, composition under Liadoff and Rimsky-Korsakoff, and conducting under Tcherepnin; in 1909 he left that august institution.

During these Conservatoire years he is credited with about a hundred compositions. Prokofieff remained in Russia till 1918, when he made his way to the United States of America, travelling via Siberia and Japan. From 1922 to 1923 he lived in Germany (Bavaria) and thereafter in France, but he has toured in many countries as pianist.

From this brief tale various inferences can be drawn with reasonable accuracy. Prokofieff is a prolific composer, and his output will probably be unequal (though he has revised many of his works and in some cases withheld publication altogether). He is a brilliant pianist and has written much for that instrument. On the one hand, the traditional art-forms; on the other, all the naive panoply of folk-song and folk-lore, with its bright colours and its melancholy, and its legends of fairy princesses, hobgoblins, and wizards. On the one hand, the classical sonata; on the other, *Baba Jaga, Le Coq d'Or*. In the difficulty of reconciling these two elements lies probably the key to Prokofieff's first period, though from the beginning he showed himself the possessor of a sardonic humour and a gift for satire wholly individual.

The second period is one of maturity, a development from and a culmination of the first, and Prokofieff now departs from Russia to America over the plains of Siberia and the exotic seas of Japan. The third period may be said to date from his return to Europe (but not to Russia).

The year 1918, then, is one of the turning-points in his career. Of what does his artistic output up to Op. 32 consist? First and foremost of a number of works for piano; four sonatas, Op. 1, 14, 28, 29; three concertos (of which more anon: the second and third are in a class by themselves); and several sets of *Klavierstücke* or *Morceaux pour piano*—*Quatre Études*, Op. 2; *Marche*, Op. 3; *Four Sketches*, Op. 4; *Toccata*, Op. 11; *Ten Sketches and Dances*, Op. 12; *Sarcasmes*, Op. 17; *Visions Fugitives* (twenty in number), Op. 22; *Incantation*, Op. 30; *Contes de la vieille grand'mère* (four in number), Op. 31; *Four Dances*, Op. 32. Two sets of songs, the one, Op. 35, without words, the other, Op. 36, to poems by Balmont, are closely-knit and concentrated, but not unvocal, and the difficulties of execution are well worth surmounting.

If we look for fresh developments of the sonata form, we are disappointed. The four examples are immature, being mostly revisions of works written by the composer in his 'teens; the third and fourth, indeed, bear the inscription *d'après les vieux cahiers*, though the former (A minor) in one movement is a vigorous and capable enough piece of writing. The smaller pieces for piano vary in merit. The *Suggestion diabolique*, Op. 4, No. 4, is fantastic and effective; the *Toccata* has a hard brilliance of its own; the delicate *Prélude*, Op. 12, No. 7, might illustrate a scene from the

Willow Pattern; the *Sarcasmes* live up to their title; what the old grandmother has to say is delightful; and the *Gavotte*, Op. 32, No. 3, is grotesquely attractive. But much of the rest somehow does not convince; one feels that the composer is out rather *pour épater le bourgeois*, and it is a jest that soon loses its savour. (It is amusing, too, to see how often the indication *feroce* is written over the music.) The influence of Liszt is apparent, both in the bravura style of writing (but brought up to date, of course) and in the preoccupation with musical diablerie, but Liszt makes a dangerous mentor for the young. There are also some sets of songs, Op. 9, 23, 27, lyrical in feeling and with a quiet beauty of their own, and an entertaining setting of Hans Andersen's Tale, *Le vilain petit canard* ('The Ugly Duckling'), Op. 18—a typical choice of subject; an *Incantation*, text by Balmont, Op. 30, for tenor, chorus and orchestra; a *Ballade* for 'cello and piano, Op. 12; a curious, spidery, but not unattractive *Concerto* for violin and orchestra, Op. 19, in three movements.

We should not, however, bewail what Prokofieff in his early years with his technique and imagination might have written, but rather congratulate ourselves on having such intriguing works as the *Suite Scythe*, the ballet *Chout*, and the second and third Piano Concertos. The *Suite Scythe* (*Ala et Lolly*), Op. 20 (1914), is scored for a large orchestra, and is a grand and barbaric affair in four movements, mostly in dance rhythm (it has, indeed, been performed as a ballet). The first movement rises to an orgy of sound; the second is a wild and furious dance; the third, a nocturne, heavy and still; the fourth, a solemn and dazzling cortège. It is a subject typically Russian —that fierce struggle for existence on the brooding steppes; warriors, born to the saddle, and with traditions going back to the Medes and Persians; a race whose food is kumiss, and whose occupation is to wander. The ballet, *Chout*, Op. 21, bearing the dates 1915 (1920) and first performed in 1921, is a farcical popular Russian tale of how a buffoon and his wife by means of practical tricks worked on the incredulity of seven other buffoons and of a rich merchant, making themselves quickly rich by the process. There are melodies in the score that might well be folk-songs, but the harmony is spicy and piquant to a degree. Those who like sipping cocktails and watching acrobats perform against clashes of colour will find *Chout* entertaining; others will deem it an unnecessary *tour de force*. The second and third Piano Concertos would make most welcome additions to the limited répertoire of the orchestral pianist. The former in G minor, Op. 16, composed in 1913, recomposed in 1923, published in 1925, is in four movements; the first lyrical but rising to fine climaxes; a rhythmic and original scherzo; a rhapsodic intermezzo; and a brilliant finale, interspersed with hints of plainsong. The third Concerto in C major, Op. 26 (1917–21), is perhaps the better of the two. It is in three movements, the first and third of which contain much clean, hard polyphonic writing, especially in the developments of the first subjects, while the second subjects are warmer and more lyrical; the second movement is in the form of an air with variations. Both these concertos are eminently pianistic; they are brilliant but not extravagant; they offer ample scope to the soloist but never descend to being mere vehicles for virtuosic display. The symphonic treatment of the themes and the actual themes themselves are full of interest and vitality, and the balance is admirably kept between the solo instrument and the orchestra.

Prokofieff's second period, one of full maturity—if it may be called a period—consists of but two works, an opera and a sextet, though the two piano concertos might be included, had they not been conceived so long before the departure of the composer for America. The outcome of this visit was a commission for an opera from the authorities in Chicago, and *L'Amour des trois Oranges*, Op. 33, was written and scored in 1919 in nine months' time, though it did not actually receive its *première* till the end of 1921. It is a satire of the eighteenth-century Venetian, Carlo Gozzi, and tells of a hypochondriac prince who can only be cured by being made to laugh. This is successfully accomplished, but a wicked witch sets a fresh spell on him and he is compelled to search for the Three Oranges. By a trick he obtains them from their awe-inspiring guardian, and inside one of them he finds the Princess Ninetta. After various adventures in which the traitors at court who are intriguing for their downfall are finally routed, the happy pair are united. It is a subject that must have made an irresistible appeal to the composer, with all its paraphernalia of magic and fairy-tale. Here Prokofieff's feeling for fantasy, his love of satire, and his marvellous technique (sharpened now through years of practice) are given full play; the orchestral writing is certainly very brilliant. The *Ouverture sur thèmes juifs,* Op. 34 (1919), for clarinet, string quartet, and piano is a short work, rich in sentiment (though of course, *sentimentality* and Prokofieff are poles apart). While *L'Amour des trois Oranges* is characterized by an exuberant luxury, here there is an exquisite restraint. The restlessness and foreboding of the children of Israel, and the dreams and aspirations of the Ghetto find here their expression, but the final five chords are bold and defiant. Scrupulous regard, too, is paid to the medium, and the scoring is crystal-like and clear.

Prokofieff can now be said to be at the height of his powers. His writing is spontaneous, not forced, and his touch is sure, but it is impossible not to believe that the impressions and experiences of America and Western Europe did not have their influence, though one need not exaggerate the importance and extent of that influence. His style becomes much less fantastic and much more intense, but that does not imply that it was formerly superficial. It becomes now definitely objective and follows the general trend of European musical thought (Stravinsky in Paris, for example), but no one can accuse Prokofieff of ever having been a romantic or of ceasing to be characteristically individual. The discord, used formerly rather as a sonority complete in itself (notably in *Chout*), now occurs logically at the meeting of different strands of melody and lines of thought, but polyphony is not a new feature of the work of this composer. Finally, American and Western European life and art—the chequer-board planning of towns, the lofty architecture, machinery, cubism, blank verse, painting either decorative or plastic—throw the straight line into high relief, cast firm shadows and make for the severe, but Prokofieff's writing was always dynamic.

Of this third period the best works are probably the Quintet for oboe, clarinet, violin, viola, and double-bass, and the Ballet, *Le Pas d'Acier*. The former, Op. 39 (1924), is in six short movements, slow and quick alternating—stern, uncompromising music. Prokofieff exploits the characteristics of the different instruments, challenges with rhythmic audacities (especially in the third movement, where the permutations and combinations of five-four time are examined), and does not fail to be ironic. *Le Pas d'Acier*, an impressive and powerful work, first produced in 1927, gives us the apotheosis of machinery. The gospel of work is preached by manual labour and machinery in the villages and factories. The corps de ballet gyrate, and describe the movements of mighty engines; the orchestra works up to a fierce climax of steam and steel, of stamping hammers, of whirring fly-wheels. But is man making the machine human, or is the machine making man mechanical? That is the problem. The Fifth Piano Sonata, Op. 38, largely an essay in polytonality, is disappointing.

Prokofieff is now just thirty-eight years old; one can hope with confidence for further masterpieces, worthy to be set beside the chamber music, the piano concertos, the ballets, and *L'Amour des trois Oranges*.